The Nanny HANDBOOK

The essential guide to being a nanny

Teena Kamen

Hodder & Stoughton
www.hodderheadline.co.uk

To my son, Tom Jennings,
with love and affection.

Orders: please contact Bookpoint Ltd, 130 Milton Park, Abingdon, Oxon OX14 4SB. Telephone: +44 (0)1235 827720. Fax: +44 (0)1235 400454. Lines are open from 9.00–6.00, Monday to Saturday, with a 24-hour message-answering service. You can also order through our website www.hodderheadline.co.uk.

British Library Cataloguing in Publication Data
A catalogue record for this title is available from the British Library

ISBN 0 340 81468 3

First published 2004
Impression number 10 9 8 7 6 5 4 3 2 1
Year   2007 2006 2005 2004

Typeset by Pantek Arts Ltd, Maidstone, Kent.
Printed in Italy for Hodder & Stoughton Educational, a division of Hodder Headline, 338 Euston Road, London NW1 3BH.

Contents

Acknowledgements

Many thanks to the Marr family and the Pinder family with whom I gained my experience of working as a nanny.

Thanks also to the pupils and staff at Rood End Primary School and Withymoor Primary School where I gained much of my experience of working with young children.

Special thanks to Rebecca Brown, Chris Helm, Terry James and Pauline White for their technical support and invaluable contributions during the writing of this book.

Picture credits

The authors and publishers would like to thank the following for permission to reproduce material in this book:

p.5, Hulton Archive/Getty Images; p.12, Richard Hamilton Smith/CORBIS; p.14, Paul Doyle/Photofusion; p.20, Melanie Friend/Photofusion; p.22, Christa Stadtler/Photofusion; p.27 and p.162, Jacky Chapman/Photofusion; p.63, John Henley/CORBIS; p.88, LWA-Stephen Welstead/CORBIS; p.97, Laura Dwight/CORBIS; p.99, Raoul Minsart/CORBIS; p.103, Topham Monika Graff Image Works; p.118, Alamy; p.122, Michael Keller/CORBIS; p.127, LWA-Dann Tardif/CORBIS; p.137, Tom Stewart/CORBIS; p.146, p.157, p.159 and p.172, Jennie Woodcock, Reflections Photolibrary/CORBIS; p.164, David Stoecklein/CORBIS; p.171, Ariel Skelley/CORBIS; p.178, John Madere/CORBIS.

Every effort has been made to obtain necessary permission with reference to copyright material. The publishers apologise if inadvertently any sources remain unacknowledged and will be glad to make the necessary arrangements at the earliest opportunity.

Introduction

This book aims to provide a detailed and comprehensive guide to all aspects of working with young children in their own home. It includes information about:

* training opportunities and qualifications
* employment issues
* establishing and maintaining positive working relationships with children and parents
* responding to possible problems and special situations within the family
* children's safety, first aid and child protection awareness
* ideas and activities relating to children's development and early learning
* providing stimulating opportunities for play
* promoting children's emotional wellbeing
* managing children's behaviour
* making the most of free time and participating in nanny networks
* travelling and working abroad
* moving into other careers working with children.

Throughout the book there are useful examples illustrating the day-to-day work of a nanny; these are based on good childcare theory and practice, as well as the experiences of real nannies.

The book also includes exercises to develop the nanny's personal and professional skills, plus activities to encourage and/or extend children's development and learning.

* What is a nanny?
* Why be a nanny?
* A brief history of the British nanny
* Types of nanny
* Other types of childcare in the home
* The role of the nanny
* Personal qualities
* Experience of working with children
* Advantages and disadvantages of working as a nanny

WHAT IS A NANNY?

A nanny provides childcare in the child's (or children's) own home, usually while the parents are at work. Employing a nanny is a particularly useful childcare option for parents who work at times when other forms of childcare are not readily available, for example, evenings, nights or weekends. A nanny has sole charge of the children, so ideally should be a skilled childcare practitioner. A qualified nanny will have gained a recognized childcare qualification (see chapter 2) relating to children from birth to eight years, including the study of:

* physical care and development
* nutrition
* health and safety
* learning through play
* children's language, intellectual, emotional and social development.

However, not all nannies are trained and, at the moment, there are no legal requirements for a person applying to work as a nanny to have any qualifications. So some nannies may have no formal qualifications in childcare, but may have a little or a lot of experience of working with young children.

A qualified and/or experienced nanny can:

* look after children of any age
* provide high quality, convenient childcare in the family home
* provide plenty of fun and learning opportunities within a safe environment
* work flexible hours to suit the family's requirements
* ensure the children are safe, well cared for and happy
* provide continuity of care and less disruption to children's home routine
* provide individual attention
* provide support to the whole family
* work full-time or part-time
* live in or live out
* meet each child's physical, emotional, social and intellectual needs
* have special childcare skills, with a clear understanding of children.

WHY BE A NANNY?

Working as a nanny can be very enjoyable because children can be so delightful, funny and creative. Great personal and professional satisfaction can be gained from helping children to develop their individual potential. However, working as a nanny can also be frustrating, extremely demanding and even exhausting. As all children are different, there will always be plenty of variety in your work. You will not earn huge sums of money working as a nanny, but in the right job, with a considerate employer, you will certainly never be bored!

Ten possible reasons for wanting to be a nanny:

1 You have a genuine love of children.
2 You enjoy children's company.
3 You enjoy working with children.
4 You enjoy assisting with children's development.
5 You prefer a one-to-one relationship with a child rather than working with a group of children in a nursery or school.
6 You want a rewarding and fulfilling career working with children and their families.
7 You want to gain valuable experience for when you bring up your own children.
8 You would like an easier transition into the world of work.
9 You want to escape from difficult or boring home circumstances.
10 You want a higher standard of living than you would usually have (e.g. as a live-in nanny you may have use of a car and/or accompany the family on holidays abroad; also you have no travelling expenses to work and no rent or mortgage to pay).

People working as nannies can usually be divided into three categories:

1 Young, single people with babysitting and/or childcare experience and who are interested in working as a nanny for a year or two. You may be taking a break from college or preparing for another career working with children (e.g. I worked as a nanny prior to my career as a primary school teacher).

2 Older, more mature people who have raised their own children and want to work in a family environment because they enjoyed caring for their own children. You may have trained and worked as a nursery nurse prior to having your own children or may have other childcare experience such as running a playgroup or being a childminder.

3 People who consider they are childcare professionals and specialists. You may have specialist nanny training or a degree in early childhood education or primary education. You consider being a nanny a lifetime career and have worked as a nanny for several years.

EXERCISE: List your own reasons for wanting to work as a nanny.

A BRIEF HISTORY OF THE BRITISH NANNY

During the Middle Ages (especially in winter when food was scarce) babies were breastfed as long as possible, until they were two or three years old. From at least the thirteenth until the eighteenth century, it was common practice for wealthy women to pay poorer women, known as wet-nurses, to breastfeed their children. In the eighteenth century the benefits of mothers breastfeeding their own children were established (e.g. breast milk was now known to protect babies against disease) and it then became common for mothers to breastfeed their own children. A wet-nurse was still hired to breastfeed a baby whose mother had died or was too ill to do it herself. Some wet-nurses stayed on after the child was weaned and were known as dry-nurses. In the nineteenth century the wet-nurse disappeared. The nanny may not have evolved from the wet-nurse, but from the dry-nurse – a child's nurse who was responsible for looking after rather than feeding the child or children.

The earliest recorded use of the term 'nanny' was in 1711, when Lady Mary Wortley Montagu wrote a letter to her old nurse addressing her as 'Dear Nanny' (Gathorne-Hardy 1972). The term 'nurse' was used in the fifteenth century to describe a woman who cared for children. The term was used commonly from that time until the nineteenth century, when the title 'nanny' appears, but was mostly used by children rather than adults. For example, the Victorians used the title 'nurse' in advertisements and domestic agencies.

Where the title 'nanny' came from is uncertain. It may originate from the word 'grandmother'. Many grandmothers are still called 'Nanny' today. It may be derived from the term 'Nursie' used in the early nineteenth century. By the 1920s, 'nanny' became universally used by both children and adults and the title was also used in advertisements instead of 'nurse'.

In the past a nanny used her own surname or took on the surname of the first family she stayed with for a long time and was known by that name for her entire career as a nanny (e.g. if the surname of the first family I worked for as a nanny was Jones, I might have been called 'Nanny Jones' and would have kept this name even when I went on to work for the Smith family.)

Nurseries existed in wealthier households from the thirteenth century. A wealthy family had a separate room or rooms for the children, that is, a nursery. As more people became richer, more people had nurseries. During the eighteenth century nurseries became increasingly common.

During the first half of the nineteenth century the traditional nursery became established. The nursery was usually situated at the very top of the house or in a distant wing, as far away as possible from the adult members of the family. The nanny was the absolute ruler within the nursery environment and slept in a room just off the nursery. Breakfast, lunch and tea were eaten in the nursery; parents ate separately in the dining room. On Sundays and special occasions such as birthdays, the children would be dressed in their Sunday best and would come down to eat lunch with their parents. Parents did not usually enter the nursery world, although they might go up to say goodnight to their children.

Mothers had a dominant role in bringing up their children until the eighteenth century. After that, children saw their mother only for a short designated period each day and were cared for by the servants, under the direction of the nanny. During the nineteenth century the nanny became established in all affluent households. It was not just the aristocracy and the gentry who hired nannies, but also wealthy tradesmen. Middle-class parents had at least a nursemaid to care for their children.

At the beginning of the twentieth century the parents of children in wealthy families, especially the aristocracy, had very little day-to-day contact with their children. The Edwardian era was the classic period of children being seen but not heard – or, better yet, not being seen at all! From birth, children in such families were brought up by nannies who often became mother substitutes. Children would see their parents for about an hour each day, usually after breakfast, to wish their parents good morning and/or after tea, for a short storytelling session.

Between the 1920s, and 1940s, middle-class mothers increasingly became more involved in bringing up their young children. Many of these families no longer employed nannies. 'Expert advice' was now available from books, magazines and special classes, such as Frederick Truby King's Mothercraft Society. During the 1920s, nursery magazines began to give advice on the upbringing of young children. For example, *Nursery World* first appeared in 1925 and is still published weekly today.

After the Second World War new ideas about childrearing became increasingly popular and were influenced by liberal ideas concerning childcare. In the 1950s

The traditional British nanny

women were encouraged to stay at home to look after their own children. Mothers were seen as being at the centre of childrearing, but fathers were also encouraged to play a more important role. Benjamin Spock's *Common Sense Book of Baby and Child Care* was first published in 1946, and during the 1950s had the most book sales apart from the Bible (Humphries *et al.* 1988).

Nannies trained other nannies. There was often a career progression, starting off with work as a nursemaid or nursery maid, then working as an under-nurse or second nanny and then either taking over from the old nanny to become head nurse/nanny or taking up a post as a nanny in a new household.

The first school for nannies was the Norland Institute, founded in 1892 by Emily Ward to train young women to care for young children. The training included learning about nursery rules and routines, needlework, cookery, art, singing and storytelling. By the 1930s the Norland curriculum also included the principles and practice of education, child psychology, nursery management, nature study, children's drawings and children's games (Gathorne-Hardy 1972). Other nursery training colleges began appearing from the early 1900s onwards (see chapter 2). From 1920 the college-trained nanny was increasingly seen, while the number of nanny-trained nannies began to decline.

From 1850, the career of the nanny became formalized, including a uniform. Before 1850, nurses and nursemaids wore the same type of clothes as other domestic servants, e.g. the head nurse/nanny dressed like a housekeeper while the nursemaid dressed like a housemaid. From 1850, as the specialist nanny became established, a uniform was developed resembling that of a hospital nurse. The nursery training colleges had their own distinctive uniforms. By the

1950s it gradually became more usual for nannies not to wear uniforms. Today nannies wear what they like (usually what is most practical for the job), although nannies trained at the specialist colleges may still wear a uniform.

In the past a career as a nanny had many benefits; although wages were small, they were adequate and usually higher than for the majority of domestic servants. In 1905 a nanny earned about £15 a year. However, especially in larger households, the nanny would not have had very much work to do, as she was assisted by other servants - such as the nursemaid, the housemaid and the cook, who provided all the meals for the nursery. The nursemaid did most of the household chores related to looking after the children and the nursery. In addition, there was usually a chauffeur to take the nanny and the children wherever they wanted to go. Nannies also went to places they would never have seen otherwise, including travelling abroad. Up until 1939 it was not uncommon for an old domestic servant to be given money or a home as a pension in retirement. A retired nanny was sometimes given the use of a house or cottage until she died; sometimes the old nanny continued living in the family house.

Today a live-in nanny earns about £190–300 per week (£280–360 in London), while a daily nanny earns approximately £210–£310 per week (£325–450 in London). The roles of the nanny and nursemaid are now combined as one. The nanny is also expected to drive the children wherever they need to go (e.g. nursery, school etc.), using their own or the family car. Travelling abroad may still be one of the benefits of working as a nanny. Now nannies have to make their own provision for pensions and retirement.

Before 1914 families were wealthier and larger, so nannies stayed longer and had greater control over the children. After the First World War nannies left families sooner and more frequently. There were closer contacts with parents, but these resulted in more conflicts between them. There was a decline in the demand for nannies in the twentieth century due to changes in social and economic structures. Despite the general decline in the employment of nannies after the Second World War, children in wealthy families continued to be brought up by nannies. Increasingly, financially successful professionals also employed nannies to fit in with their working patterns and their need for more flexible childcare arrangements.

In the twenty-first century there is now an increasing demand for nannies (and other forms of childcare), due to the fact that more women (including those with very young children) work outside the home. The statistics on working mothers shown below provide a good example:

✳ 20% of women with dependent children work full-time

✳ 36% of women with pre-school children work part-time

✳ 56% of women whose youngest child was under five were working in 2002

✳ 79% of women whose youngest child was aged 11-15 were working in 2002

✳ 57% of lone mothers (compared to 77% of lone fathers) were working in 2002.

(NFPI, October 2003)

In many families both parents work and many have jobs with long and/or unsociable hours, e.g. vets, doctors, nurses and others in the emergency services, as well as shop or hotel managers and others in the food and leisure industries. Almost two-thirds of working families contain a parent who works outside the traditional Monday-to-Friday, nine-to-five pattern.

However, parents with young children who work more traditional hours may still have problems with access to childcare. In 2003 there was only one childcare place for every seven children under the age of eight (NFPI 2003).

It is not just wealthy families who hire nannies; many middle-income couples do so as well. Many couples enjoy the lifestyle that two incomes can bring. Many women have established careers that they do not want to give up. For many families, it is an economic necessity for both parents to work. If they can afford it they may choose to employ a nanny. High-flying single parents may also require (and can afford) the flexible childcare that is offered by a nanny rather than the restricted hours of a day nursery.

It is not just working mothers who hire nannies; some full-time mothers (or fathers) may also do so for a variety of reasons:

❋ they may not need to work as they have inherited money or have a wealthy spouse

❋ they may need to support their spouse's job (e.g. politician or businessman), including entertaining VIPs/clients and travelling abroad

❋ they may be involved in charity work and fundraising.

In the past British nannies also worked abroad, employed by foreign upper-class families. Before the First World War there were many British nannies in Austria. Before the Russian Revolution there were many British nannies working in Russia. Between the two world wars British nannies were popular in France. Before the Spanish Civil War most families in the Spanish aristocracy employed British nannies (Gathorne-Hardy 1972).

Today the British nanny is still highly sought-after, but strict employment laws in most countries prevent many from working abroad, although there are plenty of opportunities to work as an au pair. British families who are living and working abroad employ most of the British nannies that work abroad.

TYPES OF NANNY

Live-in nanny

Live-in nannies live with the family they are working for, with food and their own bedroom (and often bathroom) included as part of their salary. Many families offer a self-contained flat for their nanny. The live-in nanny is expected to work five days a week. Usual working hours are from breakfast-time until bath-time (e.g. 7.30 a.m. to 7 p.m.), with negotiable babysitting. A live-in nanny should not work more than 12 hours a day (excluding evening babysitting). A live-in nanny needs to be flexible about babysitting and available for one or two nights a week, as agreed with the parents. It is usual for a live-in nanny to receive two full days off every week. Holidays are negotiable, although four weeks' paid holiday is the norm.

Live-out/daily nanny

The live-out or daily nanny comes to the family home each day only for the hours of work. The daily nanny looks after the children during working hours (usually 8 a.m. to 6 p.m.) for five days a week, although there should be room for flexibility. A daily nanny should not work for more than ten hours a day. Babysitting in the evenings might be arranged as part of the terms of employment or in exchange for extra pay, e.g. as paid overtime. Holidays are upon agreement, although the standard is four weeks' paid holiday per year. Salaries for a daily nanny are far higher than for a live-in nanny, particularly in London and the South-east, because they have to pay for their own accommodation and living expenses.

Nanny-share

A nanny-share is an arrangement where one nanny looks after the children from two families, either at the same time or by dividing time between the two. A nanny who looks after the children of more than two families must be registered as a childminder.

There are several different types of nanny-shares:

* complete share: children cared for together by the nanny five days a week
* part-time share: children cared for together two to three days a week by the nanny
* split-week share: children cared for separately by the nanny, e.g. half the week with one family and half the week with another
* main family share: nanny works full time for one family and cares for children from another family for part of the week.

A nanny-share can be a more economical way of employing a nanny and is also particularly useful for working parents with school-age children. A nanny-share is usually arranged on a live-out basis, unless one family decides to have the nanny living in while the other family pays half the wages/tax and contributes towards the live-in family's additional expenses.

Special-needs nanny

A special needs nanny looks after a child with special needs who has a condition or illness that means they require additional care. Special needs range from mild learning difficulties (e.g. dyslexia) to profound/multiple physical, sensory or mental disabilities. Every child is a unique individual with different needs; however, children with special needs require particular assistance to help them reach their full potential. A special-needs nanny may require special training and/or experience for specific conditions/disorders, e.g. gastronomy feeding, Makaton or British Sign Language. Working as a special-needs nanny can be more demanding physically and emotionally and may be more stressful and involve greater responsibility, but it can also be more rewarding and satisfying.

Temporary nanny

A temporary nanny is a qualified and/or experienced nanny who is available at short notice to provide parents with short-term or emergency childcare. A temporary nanny must be flexible and be prepared to work on a live-in or live-out basis. Work as a temporary nanny can last from a day to a few months. Temporary nannies may be employed when the family's normal nanny arrangements are unavailable, e.g. the nanny is ill, goes on holiday or leaves without adequate notice.

Many nannies enjoy temporary work as it offers:

✳ higher rates of pay

✳ greater flexibility

✳ more freedom and diversity

✳ less friction with employers

✳ more detachment from children

✳ opportunities to gain lots of varied experience.

Male nanny

Only 2 per cent of workers in the childcare industry (including nursery nurses, childminders, out-of-school club workers and nannies) are men. Male nannies are becoming increasingly popular, especially among working single mothers who want male role models for their children (Hinsliff, *The Observer*, 9 March 2003).

Colleges offering childcare courses have reported a small increase in the number of enquires by men; a few years ago they received none at all. It is rare to find men on traditional training courses for nannies, but attitudes are changing. Recently Norland enrolled its first full-time British male student, a 19-year-old from Wales, who wears a specially designed uniform with a navy blazer and grey trousers (Gibson, *The Observer*, 23 March 2003).

Many agencies are still reluctant even to register male nannies because it is so difficult to place them; families rarely request a male nanny. Some families do not like the idea of a young man in the role of a nanny and may be suspicious of the reasons why he wants to work with young children (e.g. concerns about paedophiles).

OTHER TYPES OF CHILDCARE IN THE HOME

Au pair

An au pair is a young single person, aged 18–27 years, from the European Union or a few other countries, e.g. within the Commonwealth. Au pairs come to the UK to study English and British culture, while living as part of a family.

In return for full board and lodging they help with the children and perform light household duties for a maximum of five hours a day or 25 hours per week. They must have at least two full days off each week, have their own room, be able to attend English classes and be given an allowance or 'pocket money'. Unlike a nanny or mother's help, an au pair does not have a contract, as the arrangement with the family is an informal one. An au pair should be treated like a member of the family rather than as an employee and receives an allowance rather than a salary. The Home Office recommends a minimum of £45 per week that must be paid to the au pair on a weekly basis.

An au pair is not a nanny and should not be considered as a nanny-substitute. Many people think that a nanny and an au pair are one and the same, but their roles are completely different. Au pairs usually have little or no formal childcare training and/or experience. An au pair should never have sole charge of babies or young children under the age of three years while the parents are out at work. Only a qualified and/or experienced nanny has sufficient skills to take on this level of responsibility. However, au pairs may be a useful option for providing after-school childcare for older children.

Mother's help

A mother's help usually works alongside the parent, helping with childcare and general household chores. Unlike nannies, mother's helps will do more general light housework, not just household duties directly related to the children. A mother's help must be at least 18 years old. Mother's helps will probably not have any formal childcare qualifications, but may have previous experience of this type of work, babysitting or looking after siblings. They may have done a childcare course at school, involving some practical experience with babies and young children in day nurseries and playgroups.

A mother's help may start by taking occasional sole charge of older children, but should not be expected to take sole charge of children under 12 months. An experienced and confident mother's help can take sole charge of the children on more occasions. Mother's helps may be a useful childcare option for parents who work from home or parents who work part-time and want general housework and childcare duties combined.

A mother's help can be employed on a live-in or live-out basis. If living in, the mother's help would expect to have her own room and to live as one of the family where possible. Some families offer to pay the travelling expenses of live-out mother's helps. A live-in mother's help should not be expected to work more than ten hours a day, although it is usual for two nights' babysitting to be included in the salary; a live-out mother's help should be paid extra for babysitting.

Maternity nurse

Maternity nurses are trained and experienced nurses or nannies who specialize in the care of newborn babies. Most maternity nurses tend to be very experienced nannies. However, some are registered nurses, ex-midwives or health visitors. Unlike nannies and mother's helps, maternity nurses are self-employed, so they are responsible for their own tax and National Insurance.

A maternity nurse will help a mother to take care of a new baby for 4–12 weeks after the birth. A maternity nurse is on call 24 hours a day, 6 days a week with one 24-hour period totally free, depending on the family's particular needs. Alternatively, a maternity nurse may be employed to work for days or nights only.

A maternity nurse is responsible for assisting a new mother with all aspects of caring for a newborn, including establishing feeding and bath-time routines as well as dealing with the baby's laundry, sterilizing bottles and preparing light meals for the mother if necessary. The maternity nurse should involve any other children in the family with the baby, but should not be expected to look after the baby's siblings as her primary responsibility is to care for the baby.

The majority of maternity nurses live with the family and sleep in the baby's room. They either take the baby to the mother for breastfeeding during the night or bottle-feed the baby themselves and then resettle the baby after a feed. They will also deal with any other needs the baby may have during the night, such as changing nappies.

Maternity nurses are particularly useful for mothers who have had twins, a difficult delivery or a caesarean. They are also useful for first-time mothers and for those who do not have friends or family nearby to provide support.

THE ROLE OF THE NANNY

A nanny's primary duties are directly related to the child or children. This involves taking care of the children's day-to-day needs in the children's own home. The exact duties will depend on the ages and individual needs of the children, as well as the specific requirements of the family. Both the nanny and the family should be clear about the precise duties expected, e.g. as specified in the job description. These duties should be formalized in the written agreement or contract (see chapter 4).

Examples of a nanny's typical duties include domestic routines, such as:

* planning and preparing regular, nutritious meals for the child, including washing up afterwards and maintaining kitchen hygiene
* feeding, changing, bathing and dressing the child, as appropriate to age and development
* keeping the fridge stocked, including food shopping for the child/family (most families do their own major food shop once a week/month and the nanny buys any additional items as necessary from the local store)
* keeping the child's bedroom clean and tidy, including changing bedding
* washing and ironing child's clothes (but should not have to wash items by hand)
* taking full charge of the house if both parents are out at work (e.g. calling a plumber if pipe bursts).

A nanny should not be responsible for general housework or chores, but should clear up after her/himself and the children, including encouraging the children to tidy up after themselves, as appropriate to age and level of development.

Nanny duties

A nanny is also responsible for identifying and meeting the child's social, intellectual and emotional needs. Examples of a nanny's typical responsibilities include:

* providing a safe and loving environment for the child
* planning stimulating activities that help the child's learning and development
* providing play activities, e.g. games, toys, arts and crafts
* providing language activities, e.g. books, stories, rhymes and songs
* providing behavioural guidelines and discipline, as agreed with the parents
* organizing outings, e.g. taking the child to the park and other places of interest.

The nanny may also be responsible for taking the child to playgroup, nursery, school, clubs, dentist or doctor, as well as outings and daytrips. This may be on foot with pushchair/pram, by car or even public transport, depending on the distances involved. Having a driving licence is an asset as it will give you more freedom to take the child out and about; you may even get use of the parental car, not only for taking the child out, but for your own private use as well (see important information about insurance in chapter 4).

Most nannies work a five-day week, usually Monday to Friday. Nannies usually have two full days off every week (e.g. the weekend), although some nannies work on Saturday mornings or a full day at the weekend by mutual agreement, in return for extra money or time off during the week. Nannies are covered by the Government's Working Time Directive limit of a working week of no more than 48 hours, although many do work as much as 50–60 hours a week. A daily nanny should not be expected to work more than ten hours a day and should be paid extra for one or two evenings' babysitting per week. A live-in nanny should not be expected to work more than 12 hours a day and will usually have one or two nights' babysitting included in the basic wage.

PERSONAL QUALITIES

Although their training and experience will be varied, all nannies should have a genuine interest in and respect for children as individuals. All nannies are unique individuals with their own distinct characteristics. However, to provide sensitive and effective support for children and their parents, a nanny should have the following personal qualities:

* cheerful and friendly disposition
* good sense of humour
* reliability and stability
* patience and kindness
* honesty and discretion
* flexibility
* confidence
* enthusiasm
* independence
* physical fitness and energy.

A successful nanny should also have these personal skills and attitudes:

* good verbal and written communication skills
* ability to listen to children and take seriously what they say
* knowledge and understanding of children's behaviour and actions
* enjoyment of children's company
* resourcefulness with effective organizational skills
* responsible attitude
* ability to cope with the emotional demands of both children and parents
* a calm approach to life
* ability to deal with children in an emergency or crisis
* creative ideas to stimulate children's imagination
* ability to gain children's respect
* willingness to work hard, including working long hours.

EXERCISE: Make a list of your own personal qualities, skills and attitudes

EXPERIENCE OF WORKING WITH CHILDREN

To find out if you have the necessary personal qualities, skills and attitudes to work as a nanny, you should spend time with children in a structured setting, e.g. doing voluntary work in a school, playgroup or after-school club. Not only will it help you to decide if working with children is for you, it will also be useful preparation for doing a childcare course.

Any experience of working with children will also help you to develop your knowledge, understanding and skills regarding the care and education of young children. The more experience you have of working with children, the more prepared you will be to deal with the demands of being a nanny; it will also give you a distinct advantage when applying for jobs, as many parents value a nanny's experience as much as training.

Examples of experience of working with children include:

* babysitting
* work experience in school, nursery etc.
* leadership involvement in guide or scout activities
* volunteer work, e.g. playgroups, parent and toddler groups
* volunteer work for charities, e.g. children with special needs
* other jobs in childcare, e.g. nursery nurse, nursery assistant, childminder.

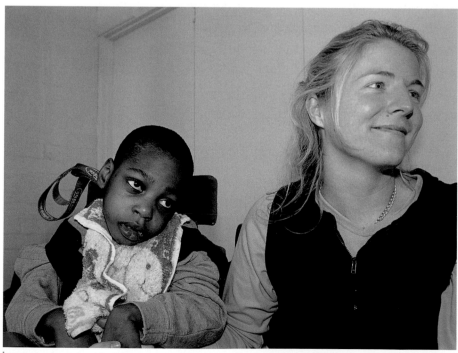

Volunteer work with children

ADVANTAGES AND DISADVANTAGES OF WORKING AS A NANNY

First, let's start by dispelling the myths about nannies. Being a nanny is not about finding a rich husband, e.g. marrying your employer, as in *The Sound of Music*! You will not be a modern-day Mary Poppins either! However, there are many advantages to working as a nanny, including more independence and flexibility than working with children in a day nursery or school, the use of a car and a mobile phone, the possibility of self-contained accommodation, travel and holidays abroad; but remember, your time will be spent mostly caring for the children, not living the high life! There are also some disadvantages, such as long hours, loneliness, isolation and the possibility of unreasonable demands, especially if you are working as a live-in nanny.

General advantages of working as a nanny:

* highly rewarding career
* working with children can be fun and entertaining
* provides an outlet for your own creative skills
* satisfaction in helping children progress to their next level of development
* varied and interesting work
* can give individual attention to the child
* working in comfortable, relaxed home environment
* more independence and flexibility than other childcare settings
* good preparation for when you have your own children!

General disadvantages of working as a nanny:

* working with children is demanding
* children can be messy, noisy and uncooperative
* working as a nanny can be exhausting, both physically and emotionally
* may be conflicting demands (e.g. between your training and the parents' wishes)
* can be stressful at times
* you may become very attached to children and will need to deal with feelings when you move on
* long hours, including babysitting and some weekend work, which can lead to loneliness and isolation
* no one to cover if you are ill, go on holiday or leave unexpectedly.

Some advantages of being a live-in nanny:

* no bills to pay, as food, light, heat, hot water, telephone and car are provided by family

- if you are a young nanny, having your own bedroom (with a TV and video to relax in away from the family) will probably be more pleasant and comfortable than a bedsit
- use of washing machine, dryer, dishwasher and hair dryer
- flexibility (although this may include being on hand to help out in a family crisis or emergency)
- no travelling to work expenses or hassles, e.g. traffic jams, bad weather.

Some disadvantages of being a live-in nanny:

- hard to live and work with other people who are not family or friends
- adapting to another family's way of life: diet, budget, manners, habits etc.
- family may not have had live-in help before
- living in someone else's home can be difficult, especially if you have previously lived in your own flat; you may find it hard to adapt to the family's routines
- deprivation of privacy for both nanny and employer
- limits to friends and boy/girlfriend visits
- may be put upon, e.g. parents may not care about being late if you live there; unscheduled babysitting may mean dropping your own plans at the last minute.

Some advantages of being a daily nanny:

- freedom and independence, which may be more important if you are a mature, more experienced nanny
- less friction with employers as more privacy
- clearer boundaries between roles of parent and nanny, which is better for all, especially the children
- babysitting duties clearer, more evenings to yourself
- days off are less awkward as you are not hanging around the family's home when you have no plans to go out
- keeps your private life private as in any other job working with children
- more businesslike arrangement as you leave after your day's work.

Some disadvantages of being a daily nanny:

- will not have the same perks of being a live-in nanny
- may have difficulties travelling to work, such as traffic jams and bad weather, which may affect your punctuality (it is essential to be punctual for employers with certain jobs, e.g. doctor or vet on call)
- must be able to give adequate notice to employer if you are ill so they can make alternative childcare arrangements (i.e. you must have a telephone).

Further reading

Gathorne-Hardy, J., 1972, *The Rise and Fall of the British Nanny*, Hodder and Stoughton.

Hobart, C. and Frankel, J., 1996, *Practical Guide to Childcare Employment*, Nelson Thornes.

Marten, S., 1997, *Careers in Child Care: your questions and answers*, Trotman.

Woolfson, R., 1997, *The Professional Nanny Handbook, Nursery World* edition, Caring Books.

Training opportunities 2

 Legal requirements

 Childcare and education qualifications

 Specialist colleges

 First aid training

 Short courses

 A professional portfolio

LEGAL REQUIREMENTS

There are no legal requirements for nannies to have any training or qualifications. However, as caring for children is a skilled and demanding job, appropriate qualifications provide you with the skills and confidence to do the job effectively and professionally. Most further education (FE) colleges offer a range of childcare and education courses (see below).

At the moment, nannies are the only childcarers who do not have some form of mandatory registration. The government has been considering responses to the consultation for a proposed Home Childcarers scheme and working out the details for such a scheme. A Home Childcarer would look after children in the home of the child's parents. Home Childcarers would be childcare professionals offering safe, good quality childcare while providing stimulating play and learning opportunities to assist the children's development. Home Childcarers would be required to meet strict criteria, as set out in a code of practice that would be monitored by Ofsted.

There are approximately 120,000 nannies working in the UK (*Early Years Educator*, November 2003). The exact number of nannies is unknown as their work is unregulated; there may be double this number working in British homes. The increasing demand for flexible and cost-effective childcare means that nannies could hold the key to the future of childcare provision, especially if plans for their registration, regulation and accreditation are implemented.

The recognition of the nanny as a registered childcarer could lead to a further increase in the number of nannies as more parents would be able to afford this type of childcare. At present parents cannot receive help towards the cost of employing a nanny, as nannies are not registered childcare providers, unlike childminders or day nurseries.

The Professional Association of Nursery Nurses (PANN) has formed a national working group to provide a forum for the identification, analysis and development of nationally recognized criteria for the work of nannies. The group also lobbies the government on introducing legislation that would require the registration and monitoring of all childcarers throughout their careers.

CHILDCARE AND EDUCATION QUALIFICATIONS

Some nannies may be unqualified, but most will have a childcare qualification, such as the Level 3 Diploma in Child Care and Education (the successor to the CACHE Diploma in Nursery Nursing, formerly known as the NNEB). A qualified nanny may also have an NVQ Level 3 in Early Years Care and Education (known previously as the NVQ Level 3 in Childcare and Education) or an Edexcel Level 3 BTEC National Diploma in Early Years (previously known as the BTEC National Diploma in Nursery Nursing). The Qualifications and Curriculum Authority provides information about these and other equivalent qualifications. New national standards for qualifications in childcare and education have been introduced and many existing qualifications have been renamed.

You can find out the latest information about these qualifications from the Early Years National Training Organization, national examining/awarding bodies, local colleges that run childcare courses in your area or local nanny agencies (see Appendix: Useful information, at the end of this book). Qualified and experienced nannies can use their childcare qualifications as a stepping stone to other courses, e.g. advanced diplomas, foundation degrees and even teacher training (see below).

EXERCISE: Find out which childcare training opportunities are available in your local area.

Qualified nannies have usually followed a two-year course covering all aspects of childcare and education, from birth to eight years of age, including:

❋ observing and assessing children's development and behaviour
❋ planning, implementing and evaluating learning activities
❋ maintaining children's safety (including first aid)
❋ equal opportunities and anti-discriminatory practice
❋ children's physical care and development
❋ children's social and emotional development
❋ children's sensory and intellectual development
❋ children's language and communication skills
❋ managing children's behaviour
❋ child protection
❋ working with parents
❋ working with colleagues and other professionals.

In addition, a college course includes written assignments/examinations and practical assessments in a variety of childcare settings, including day nurseries, nursery units/schools and primary schools. A childcare and education qualification gives parents the reassurance that you are committed to a career as a childcare professional, as well as demonstrating that you have training and experience in good practice in areas such as nutrition, child development and learning through play.

Student at work placement in an early years setting

Level 2 childcare and education qualifications

Level 2 childcare and education qualifications are really only suitable for childcare professionals working under supervision, e.g. a nursery assistant working in a day nursery. However, some people working as nannies may have a Level 2 qualification, such as:

* CACHE Level 2 Certificate in Child Care and Education
* CACHE Level 2 Certificate in Early Years Care and Education
* NVQ Level 2 in Early Years Care and Education (England, Wales and Northern Ireland)
* SVQ Level 2 in Early Years Care and Education (Scotland)
* Foundation Modern Apprenticeship in Early Years Care and Education.

Studying for a Level 2 qualification can be a useful starting point for a career working with young children, especially if you:

* have limited experience of working with children
* are uncertain of which aspects of working with children appeal to you
* lack the academic skills or entry requirements for a Level 3 course (see below).

After successfully completing a Level 2 qualification you could:

* continue your studies with a Level 3 qualification
* move directly to employment, e.g. work as a mother's help
* study for an NVQ Level 3 qualification while working as a nursery assistant
* study for a Level 3 qualification at a later date.

Level 3 childcare and education qualifications

As a nanny works with young children in an unsupervised capacity, ideally you should have a Level 3 qualification. Examples of the main Level 3 childcare and education qualifications include:

* CACHE Level 3 Diploma in Child Care and Education
* Edexcel Level 3 BTEC National Certificate or Diploma in Early Years
* NVQ Level 3 in Early Years Care and Education (England, Wales and Northern Ireland)
* SVQ Level 3 in Early Years Care and Education (Scotland)
* LCCIEB NVQ Level 3 Early Years Care and Education
* Advanced Modern Apprenticeship in Early Years Care and Education
* CACHE Level 3 Diploma in Early Years Practice
* NVQ Level 3 Certificate in Work with Children APEL (Accreditation of Prior Experience and Learning).

Entry requirements for Level 3 childcare and education courses are set out below.
CACHE does not set any formal entry requirements for the Diploma in Child Care and Education (DCE), but you will need to demonstrate that you have a

satisfactory level of general education in order to cope with the demands of the diploma's written work (e.g. observations, activity plans, assignments and examinations). A GCSE grade C or above in English and one or more additional subjects is often a college requirement, especially in areas where demand for places on the diploma course is high. Successful completion of the Certificate in Early Years Care and Education (CCE) or an equivalent Level 2 qualification may be considered by some colleges.

BTEC National courses are more academic and four or five GCSEs at grade C or above (one of which must be English Language) are usually required. A GNVQ at Intermediate Level or NVQ Level 2 in Early Years Care and Education or equivalent qualification may also be acceptable to some colleges.

The entry requirements on any childcare course may be waived for mature applicants with appropriate experience (e.g. caring for their own children, working in a playgroup or as a childminder), as long as they have a satisfactory interview.

NVQ/SVQ courses and the Advanced Modern Apprenticeship involve assessment in the workplace, and student nursery nurses have their performance assessed against the National Occupational Standards for Early Years Care and Education. Applicants for such courses usually have no formal entry requirements as there are no assignments or examinations. However, if you decide to do an NVQ qualification, do not underestimate the demands of the course as there will still be some written work, e.g. writing and evaluating activity plans.

Remember, whichever childcare course you study, you will be encouraging all aspects of young children's development and learning, including language, literacy and numeracy skills. You need to be reasonably proficient in these skills yourself in order to provide effective support. However, do not worry if there are some areas in which you feel less competent; all colleges will help students with key skills such as literacy, numeracy and IT.

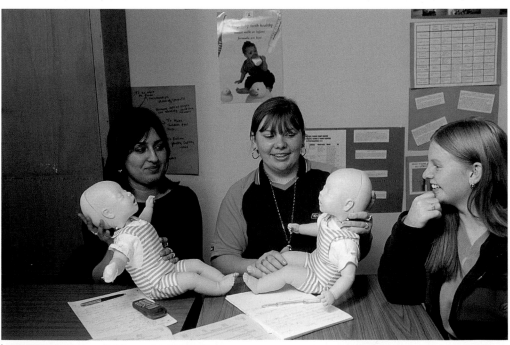

Students studying a childcare course at college

Whatever the entry requirements for a particular childcare course, you will need to attend an interview where you should show that you have a genuine interest in working with young children and that you can meet the demands of the course.

Police checks on childcare students

As a student on a childcare course you will need a Criminal Records Bureau (CRB) check because you will be involved in work placements with children. This is a legal requirement for anyone with regular, continuous and close access to children, including volunteers and students working in schools, nurseries and other day-care settings. You should not worry too much, as your college will help you with this. However, once you begin work as a nanny you will need to sort out a disclosure by yourself or through a nanny employment agency. (There is more about the CRB and disclosures in chapter 4.)

Medical checks for childcare students

Colleges may also require medical checks for all students on childcare courses. This is to safeguard both your health and that of the children you will be working with on placements. The medical check usually involves completing a simple health questionnaire, with relevant details such as your doctor's name and address, your vaccination details from childhood and/or travel immunizations. If necessary, an appointment may be made for you to see the college nurse or doctor, where they will go over your medical history, e.g. any previous or existing medical conditions such as asthma, diabetes, severe allergies. Your blood pressure is checked and details of your height and weight are recorded. A medical condition or disability will not prevent you from studying a childcare course; the college needs this information to help provide you with any additional support that you may require under the Special Educational Needs and Disability Act 2000. This Act also makes it unlawful for colleges to discriminate against disabled applicants or students.

Other career opportunities and further studies

As well as working as a nanny, a Level 3 childcare qualification can lead to employment in the following areas:

* nursery nurse
* nursery supervisor
* crèche leader
* playgroup leader
* childminder
* children's holiday representative.

You can also progress to studying higher qualifications, such as:

* CACHE Advanced Diploma in Child Care and Education
* BTEC Higher National Certificate or Diploma in Early Years Care and Education
* NVQ Level 4 in Early Years Care and Education (England, Wales and Northern Ireland)
* SVQ Level 4 in Early Years Care and Education (Scotland)
* Foundation Degree in Early Childhood Studies.

Depending on individual university and college entry requirements, you may be able to progress into nursing, teaching or other related areas of higher education (HE). (Further information on other careers working with children is in chapter 12.)

EXERCISE: What childcare qualifications and/or experience do you have already? What childcare qualification(s) are you currently studying or would you like to study?

SPECIALIST COLLEGES

Most childcare courses are available at FE colleges, but training is also available at private specialist colleges, including Norland and Chiltern. These colleges specialize in training and preparing their students for work as nannies in family homes as well as a variety of childcare settings. Their courses last for two years, during which time the students study a nationally recognized childcare qualification: the CACHE Level 3 Diploma in Child Care and Education and/or NVQ Level 3 in Early Years Care and Education. This is usually followed by a probationary period of 6–12 months, the successful completion of which leads to the college's own specialist certificate.

As these are private colleges, you would have to pay your own fees and these are very expensive (e.g. tuition fees alone are about £7000 per year, with accommodation, meals and use of college facilities incurring additional fees). Although the fees are high, you are virtually guaranteed employment and can command a much larger salary as a successful graduate from these colleges, and places are therefore in great demand.

Norland College

Norland College is probably the most well known of the specialist childcare colleges and Norland Nannies, with their traditional brown uniforms, are famous throughout the world. Emily Ward founded the Norland Institute in

1892. She believed that the care of children should be child-centred and that as well as a love of children, Norland students should have a range of practical skills (such as sewing and cooking nutritious meals for children) to enable them to provide professional, nurturing childcare; these skills are still part of the Norland curriculum today.

Norland College is now based in Bath, having moved from its previous base in Hungerford in January 2003. Since its move to Bath, Norland no longer offers residential courses, but the college has appointed a local letting agency to help students find appropriate accommodation.

Norland College offers a range of childcare courses, including:

✳ Norland Diploma in Childcare and Education
✳ Diploma of Higher Education in Early Childhood Studies
✳ Norland International Diploma Course
✳ Montessori Stage 2 Certificate: Montessori Theory and Methodology
✳ International Diploma in Montessori Pedagogy
✳ Foundation Degree in Early Years.

In addition to practical placements in a variety of childcare settings around Bath, Norland students gain practical experience of 24-hour residential childcare through short placements with local families, which is invaluable to those considering a professional career as a nanny. The Diploma of Higher Education in Early Childhood Studies is a more academic course than the Norland Diploma and students must have two A levels or Advanced GNVQ to apply.

Following the completion of a two-year diploma course at Norland, students undertake a one-year probationary period of paid employment in a childcare setting approved by the college. After successful completion of this probationary period, Norland graduates are awarded the Norland Diploma and badge.

Norland College's own in-house employment agency has a list of potential employers and works with Norland graduates to place them in their preferred type of employment, be it full-time, part-time or temporary nannies, maternity nurses, nursery nurses in nursery/primary schools and day nurseries or working abroad.

Norland College also has its own professional register for Norland graduates. The college disciplinary committee can remove from this register any Norland nursery nurses who breach the Norland College Code of Professional Conduct. Removal from the register means that they are no longer entitled to refer to themselves as Norlanders and cannot obtain work through the college's employment agency.

The Chiltern College

The Chiltern College trains residential and non-residential students to work as childcare professionals, including nursery nurses and nannies. The Chiltern College opened in 1931 and is situated in Caversham, Reading. It is now the only residential childcare training college in the UK.

Students at the Chiltern College follow a two-year course, studying either the CACHE Diploma in Child Care and Education or the NVQ Level 3 Early

Years Care and Education. Chiltern students gain practical experience in the college's on-site nurseries and school. The college also has links with local nurseries, primary schools, health visitors and hospitals.

Chiltern students study the Chiltern Certificate alongside their main award. The Chiltern Certificate includes additional theory and practice, with students spending more time on practical skills such as cooking for children and making toys from textiles and wood. Students also receive additional practical training alongside qualified and experienced staff before spending four weeks on special placements with local families where there are multiple births, to gain experience of caring for newborn babies. Chiltern students are awarded the Chiltern Certificate and badge after successfully applying their skills in a childcare setting and must have good references from a six-month period of employment to qualify.

The Chiltern College runs a graduate support scheme that provides advice and support for its graduates throughout their careers as childcare professionals.

The Chiltern College also offers an International Postgraduate Diploma. This one-year residential course is aimed at students with an early years qualification from another country who wish to gain knowledge and understanding of childcare and education in English childcare settings and also includes opportunities for students to develop their own spoken and written English.

Montessori Centre International

The Montessori Centre International is the largest Montessori training organization in the UK. It incorporates the Montessori St Nicholas Centre (established by Maria Montessori in 1946) and the London Montessori Centre (established in 1971).

Maria Montessori was an Italian educator and physician who became one of the best known and most influential early childhood educators. She began by working with children with special needs. She designed carefully graded self-teaching materials that stimulated children's learning through use of their senses. Montessori believed that children learn best by doing things independently without adult interference and that they concentrate better when engaged in self-chosen activities. Adults working with young children need to be specially trained to give the appropriate support to children's independent learning. The learning environment was considered to be particularly important. Montessori believed the equipment should be specifically designed for children (e.g. small, child-sized furniture, kitchen utensils, tools) and that children should have freedom to move and explore their environment.

Montessori courses cover all aspects of childcare, including nutrition, health and children's sensory, intellectual and creative development. The Montessori approach to childcare emphasizes the education of the whole child and the importance of independent learning.

Central to the Montessori methodology are the specialized Montessori learning materials – carefully designed and beautifully made equipment used to encourage young children's development, knowledge, understanding and practical skills.

Examples of Montessori learning materials

The Montessori Centre International offers a range of full-time courses based in London, part-time courses in Montessori centres around the UK and distance-learning programmes in the UK as well as many countries around the world. Its courses lead to internationally recognized Montessori qualifications, including:

* Stage 1 Certificate: Montessori Theory
* Stage 2 Certificate: Montessori Theory and Methodology
* Nursery Foundation Teaching Diploma
* International Diploma in Montessori Pedagogy.

Professionally trained Montessori nursery nurses can work as nannies or in a variety of childcare settings, including private or local authority nursery schools and day nurseries.

FIRST AID TRAINING

Nannies may have training in general first aid and/or paediatric first aid through their initial childcare qualification or through attending British Red Cross or St. John Ambulance courses.

British Red Cross first aid training includes:

* Practical First Aid Certificate
* Standard First Aid Certificate
* First Aid for Babies and Children
* S/NVQ in First Aid.

St. John Ambulance first aid training includes:

* Lifesaver First Aid Course
* Lifesaver Plus First Aid Course
* Lifesaver Babies and Children First Aid Course
* Early Years First Aid.

Even if you have done first aid as part of your childcare training, remember that your first aid certificate should be updated every three years.

EXERCISE: Have you got an up-to-date first aid certificate? If not, find out about the first aid courses available in your local area.

SHORT COURSES

Many nannies are keen to improve their skills and acquire further qualifications relevant to working with young children. Your employer may offer you training opportunities by arranging attendance on a first aid course or allowing you time off to go to college for childcare and education qualifications. You may wish to update your knowledge and skills through short courses available in your local area. These might include:

* paediatric first aid
* food handling and hygiene
* health and safety
* child protection awareness
* managing children's behaviour
* children with special needs.

Paediatric first aid

All adults working with babies and children should have first aid training. If you have no formal first aid qualifications, need to update your first aid skills or require additional first aid training in relation to babies and young children, you should do a paediatric first aid course. First aid protocols are different for babies and children under seven, so it is essential that you do a course that covers first aid training specific to babies and young children. A paediatric first aid course will usually include:

* introduction to first aid
* what to do in an emergency (including when to call for medical assistance)

* recognition of injuries (medical history, symptoms, signs)
* dealing with an unconscious casualty
* checking vital signs (airway, breathing, circulation)
* recovery position
* performing cardiopulmonary resuscitation (CPR) on babies and young children
* breathing difficulties (e.g. choking, asthma attack, drowning)
* circulation disorders (e.g. fainting, shock)
* head injuries (e.g. levels of response, concussion)
* severe bleeding
* minor bleeding
* precautions (e.g. gloves, tetanus, HIV and Hepatitis B awareness)
* childhood medical conditions (e.g. infantile convulsions, epileptic fits, severe allergic reactions, diabetes)
* common childhood minor and major injuries (e.g. stings and bites, burns and scalds, fractures).

For the most comprehensive and essential first aid training you should contact the British Red Cross or St. John Ambulance (see Appendix: Useful information).

Food handling and hygiene

The Basic Food Hygiene Certificate is an essential qualification for all food and beverage handlers (including nannies and childminders) and covers the basic principles of safe food handling. Many colleges include this certificate as part of their childcare and education programmes. If you do not have this certificate already, the course is available at most local colleges and includes:

* food poisoning trends and reasons
* bacteria and micro-organisms
* personal hygiene
* food safety legislation
* pest control
* cleaning and disinfecting.

Health and safety

There are several health and safety courses that are suitable for childcare professionals, including nannies. A basic course, such as the Foundation Certificate in Health and Safety, includes:

* accident prevention
* electricity
* fire safety

* first aid
* hazardous substances
* health and safety law
* manual handling
* occupational health
* safety and welfare
* work equipment.

Other short courses and workshops may also be available. Check with your local college and other training providers for courses on:

* child safety awareness
* cot death awareness
* meningitis awareness
* recognizing and preventing childhood illnesses
* baby massage
* health and nutrition.

Child protection awareness

All childcare and education courses include information on child protection, including signs and symptoms of possible child abuse, legislation, policies and procedures. If you are an unqualified nanny or need to update your knowledge in this area, you can find out about child protection through courses at your local college or distance-learning programmes, such as NSPCC Child Protection Awareness. This short course includes:

* understanding the basics of child protection
* recognizing the possible signs and indicators of child abuse
* dealing with concerns about a child's welfare
* reporting child abuse
* good practice in protecting children.

(More detailed information about first aid, hygiene, health, nutrition, children's safety and child protection is provided in chapter 7.)

Managing children's behaviour

Childcare and education courses include information on managing children's behaviour. However, if you are an unqualified nanny or have limited experience of managing children's behaviour, you might find it helpful to study a short course at your local college. A short course on managing children's behaviour will usually include:

* identifying age-appropriate behaviour
* recognizing common causes of challenging behaviours

* promoting positive behaviour
* setting goals and boundaries
* responding to unwanted behaviour
* seeking specialist advice.

(Detailed information about managing children's behaviour is provided in chapter 9.)

Children with special needs

If you care for a child with special needs, specialist training may be provided. You may be working alongside other professionals, such as a speech and language therapist, physiotherapist or occupational therapist, who can help you to learn new skills as well as provide information about relevant training. Local charities and volunteer organizations may be able to provide information and advice on specific special needs. The Montessori Centre International also offers seminars and workshops on special educational needs.

EXERCISE: Find out which short courses are available in your local area (e.g. paediatric first aid, food handling and hygiene, health and safety, child protection awareness, managing children's behaviour, children with special needs).

A PROFESSIONAL PORTFOLIO

All nannies (whether qualified or not) should prepare and organize a professional portfolio. Preparing your portfolio in advance, with all the necessary documentation, will save you time when you are registering with a nanny agency or applying for jobs. (There is more detailed information about preparing and organizing a professional portfolio in chapter 3.)

EXERCISE: Start collecting any relevant certificates and other information in preparation for organizing your professional portfolio.

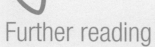

Further reading

Abbott, L. and Moylett, H. (eds.), 1997, *Working with the Under Threes: training and professional development*, Open University Press.

Beaver, M. and Brewster, J., 2002, *Babies and Young Children: Certificate in Child Care and Education*, Nelson Thornes.

Beith, K. *et al.*, 2002, *Diploma in Child Care and Education: student handbook*, Heinemann Educational.

Beith, K. *et al.*, 2003, *S/NVQ Level 2 Early Years Care and Education: student handbook*, Heinemann Educational.

Bruce, T. and Meggitt, C., 2002, *Child Care and Education*, 3rd edition, Hodder and Stoughton.

Bulman, K. and Tassoni, P., 1999, *S/NVQ Level 3 Early Years Care and Education: student handbook*, Heinemann Educational.

Green, S., 2002, *BTEC National Early Years*, Nelson Thornes.

Jones, M., 2003, *Gaining your NVQ Level 3 in Early Years Care and Education*, Scholastic.

Neaum, S. *et al.*, 2001, *Babies and Young Children: Diploma in Child Care and Education*, Nelson Thornes.

Tassoni, P., 2002, *Certificate in Child Care and Education: student handbook*, Heinemann Educational.

Finding employment 3

- Where to look for employment as a nanny
- How to apply for a job as a nanny
- References
- Your professional portfolio
- Preparing for interviews
- Questions you might be asked at interview
- Important issues to discuss at interview
- After the interview

WHERE TO LOOK FOR EMPLOYMENT AS A NANNY

There are many places you can look for employment as a nanny, including nanny recruitment agencies, advertisements in newspapers or specialist magazines, childcare colleges, local networks and the Internet.

Nanny recruitment agencies

When looking for employment as a nanny you can start by registering with a nanny recruitment agency. You can find nanny agencies by looking in the Yellow Pages, in specialist magazines such as *Nursery World* and *The Lady* or on the Internet. There are many nanny agencies to choose from, especially in cities and larger towns. A recommendation for a good nanny agency from a friend who has used one successfully can be helpful in deciding which one to choose.

By law, employment agencies cannot charge prospective employees a fee for their services. The agency charges potential employers either a fixed fee or a percentage of the nanny's salary. A reputable agency will carefully vet potential nannies and should follow the guidelines set up by the Department for Education and Skills, including interviewing each nanny on their books, carrying out the relevant background checks and ensuring that the nanny is properly qualified to work with children.

A reputable nanny agency should:

* ask you to complete a registration form and a detailed application form
* invite you for an interview (you will need to take proof of your identity – a passport, full driving licence and birth certificate – and your qualification certificates)
* apply on your behalf for an Enhanced Disclosure from the Criminal Records Bureau if you do not already have one (they are allowed to charge you a fee for this service, but it is worth doing as you will receive a copy of the disclosure, which you can use each time you apply for a new job or register with a different agency)
* try to match your requirements to suitable families who will then interview you.

To get the most out of being registered with a nanny agency, remember the following points:

* Make sure the agency has all the relevant information to assist you in your search for work. Attend an interview at the agency (if offered) so that you can discuss your requirements in greater detail and build a rapport with the agency staff.
* Keep in regular contact by telephoning the agency once a week to let them know that you are still available for work.
* Be flexible about the location of any potential nanny position; you will find work more easily if you do not restrict yourself to a specific area. You should also consider factors such as pay, conditions, working environment or the personality of a particular family, which may be more important than location.
* Let the agency know when you find work and have accepted a nanny position.

Advertisements

Parents wishing to employ a nanny may decide to advertise in a national/local newspaper or a specialist magazine. There are two main specialist magazines that include advertisements for those looking for work as a nanny: *Nursery World* and *The Lady*. *Nursery World* is the UK's only weekly magazine for early years professionals and advertises a variety of job vacancies for nursery nurses, including nanny positions. *The Lady* is England's oldest weekly magazine for women and advertises job opportunities in the domestic sector, including nannies. (Nanny recruitment agencies also regularly advertise in this magazine.)

The advertisement will include details of hours, duties, ages of children and the area where they live. Prospective nannies are usually requested to apply in writing to a box number (via the newspaper/magazine or local post office), including details of their age, experience, qualifications, employment history and a covering letter explaining why they would like to apply for this particular position.

> **KINGSWINFORD** Sole charge Nanny required from July to care for 3-year-old boy. Mon to Fri 8.00am – 6.00pm plus 1 evening babysitting. Live-in or out. Child care qualification and experience preferred. Non-smoker. Confident driver. Please write with CV to Box No. __

Example advertisement for a nanny job

Childcare colleges

You may find advertisements for nanny jobs on your college noticeboard towards the end of your childcare training or you could contact local colleges of further education that offer childcare and education courses to see if they have details of any suitable vacancies. If you are a graduate from a specialist childcare college, you can often find work through it, e.g. Norland College has its own in-house employment agency.

Local networks

Another way to find a nanny job is through local networks. Parents often put advertisements for nannies on noticeboards in local libraries, nurseries, primary schools, shops selling children's books, toys or clothes, and places where children's activities are held. This is also a good place to look if you are interested in a nanny-share. The local National Childbirth Trust group may also run a nanny-share register. You can also find work as a nanny by word of mouth, e.g. hearing about nanny vacancies through your family, friends or colleagues.

The Internet

The Internet offers a wide choice of nanny jobs, including opportunities for working abroad. Parents and nannies can advertise on the Internet through websites (such as www.nannyjob.co.uk or www.greatcare.co.uk). There are also many online nanny agencies. Nursery World Jobs has a number of nanny vacancies on the web, advertising hundreds of UK and overseas jobs. Advertisements published in the printed edition of *Nursery World* also appear on the Nursery World Jobs website for 14 days (www.jobs.nursery-world.com).

EXERCISE: Have a look at the nanny jobs available in your area:

* find local nanny recruitment agencies in the Yellow Pages
* look in the local newspaper or specialist magazines
* check your college noticeboard or contact the local college
* look at some nanny vacancies on the Internet.

HOW TO APPLY FOR A JOB AS A NANNY

Once you have found a job vacancy that meets your requirements, you need to apply for it. You need to make your application as interesting, neat and concise as possible so that the potential employer will decide to invite you for an interview. The employer will use written applications to assess which applicants best match their requirements for a nanny. From their assessments they will then prepare a shortlist of people to interview. The objective of your initial application (whether by letter or telephone) is to get an interview.

Making a written application for a job can involve:

❋ completing an application form

❋ writing a covering letter (emphasizing your suitability for this particular job)

❋ preparing a standard employment history (or curriculum vitae).

Completing an application form

If you are registering with a nanny agency you will be asked to complete an application form.

An agency will often make judgements about prospective nannies based on the way they complete their application form. The agency will not be impressed by an application form which is incomplete, difficult to read, vague, unconvincing or appears to have been completed without careful thought and attention.

When completing a nanny agency application form, remember the following important points:

1 Read carefully all the information/questions on the form and make sure you understand what is required.

2 Put the right information in the right place.

3 Photocopy the blank application form so you can draft your answers in rough first. When you are satisfied with your answers you can then copy them onto the original.

4 Use every space on the form effectively; a neat layout creates a good impression.

5 Write clearly and legibly.

6 Check your spelling and grammar.

7 Answer any questions on what you do in your spare time by giving a brief description of your main hobbies and interests rather just making a long list.

8 Be concise.

9 Make sure you give details of referees with their addresses and telephone numbers.

10 Enclose a short covering letter, highlighting any points that are especially relevant to your employment as a nanny.

11 Include any copies of certificates of qualification, references or testimonials that you hold. Never send the original certificate or diploma to anyone; if lost they can be impossible to replace. Take originals of certificates and any written references with you to your interview with the agency (or family) so that copies may be made from them.

12 Keep a copy of your application form so that you can refer to it if you are invited for an interview.

Personal details

Name: .... Date of birth: .... Age: ....

Address: ....

....

Telephone no.: .... Mobile no: ....

Email address: .... National insurance no.: ....

Nationality: .... Religion: ....

Emergency contact information
Name, address and telephone number of your next of kin (e.g. parent, spouse or partner) ....

....

Please tick Yes or No for the following:

✳ Do you have a special diet? Yes/No
✳ Would you consider yourself to be in good health? Yes/No
✳ Do you require any medication? Yes/No If yes, what?
✳ Do you have any known allergies? Yes/No If yes, what?
✳ Do you have any disabilities? Yes/No If yes, what?
✳ Are you a smoker? Yes/No
✳ Do you have a full, clean driving licence? Yes/No
✳ Are you a car owner? Yes/No If yes, is your car insured for business use? Yes/No
✳ Do you have a valid passport? Yes/No

Are you a qualified nursery nurse? Yes/No

If yes, how many years' experience do you have? ....

Type of nanny position required (please tick all that apply):
Daily   Live-in   Full-time   Part-time
Permanent   Temporary   Nanny-share   Special needs

Would you be interested in any other types of childcare positions?
Nursery work   Mother's help   Maternity nurse   Babysitting

Do you require a position offering use of a car? Yes/No

Do you have your own children? Yes/No If yes, what are their ages? ....

Will you be taking them to work with you? Yes/No

Would you be happy to work around pets? Yes/No

What ages of children do you prefer to work with?
0–12 months   1–3 years   3–5 years   5–8 years   8–11 years   11+ years

Please state the minimum salary you require: ....

Education and qualifications
Secondary school: ....
GCSEs/O Levels/CSEs: ....
A Levels: ....
College/University: ....
Course(s) studied: ....
Qualifications achieved: ....

Do you have an up-to-date first aid certificate? Yes/No

Employment history

Please give details of your current position and your previous three positions. If you are a newly qualified nursery nurse, please state your current/final college work placement and any other relevant childcare experience, e.g. babysitting, summer play schemes, voluntary work with children.

Have you given/been given notice to leave your current employer? Yes/No

From	To	Position held and ages of children	Main duties and salary	Reason for leaving

If yes, when? .... If no, what notice period is required? ....

What is the earliest date you are able to start a new position? ....

References

Please give details of the names, addresses (including postcodes) and telephone numbers of your referees, stating what position you held, duties involved, number and ages of children and how long your service for them lasted.

Name of referee	Address and telephone no.	Position held and ages of children	From	To

Disclosures

Do you have a criminal record? Yes/No

Do you have a disclosure from the Criminal Records Bureau? Yes/No
If yes, please state type and date of issue: ....

An Enhanced Disclosure is required for all applicants. If you do not have one already, do you consent to completing the necessary form? Yes/No

Additional information

Do you sing and/or play any musical instruments? Yes/No

Do you speak any other languages? Yes/No

Do you swim? Yes/No

What do you like to do in your spare time? ....
....

Signed: .... Dated: ....

Sample nanny application form

Writing a covering letter

When replying to advertisements you may be asked to apply in writing, enclosing your curriculum vitae. Or you may be asked to submit a letter of application, following an initial telephone enquiry.

The important points for completing application forms should also be remembered when applying for a job by letter. Your letter should be neatly handwritten rather than word-processed, as many employers prefer to get a sense of a prospective employee's personality by looking at their handwriting. A handwritten letter also shows a potential employer that you have taken the trouble to respond personally to their advertisement rather than simply printing out duplicate applications.

Here is an example of a covering letter:

24 July 2004

Dear Mr and Mrs Smith,

I am writing in response to your advertisement for a nanny to look after your three-year-old son.

I am a qualified nursery nurse currently working for a professional couple, caring for their two lively young sons in Stourbridge. The youngest boy will be starting school full-time in September and my employment with the family is due to end then. I enjoy working as a nanny very much as it provides many opportunities to promote young children's development, including regular outings to the swimming pool, parks, gardens, museums etc. As for things to keep the children well stimulated at home, my training as a nursery nurse enables me to provide plenty of play and early learning activities. I am very keen on the importance of sharing books with young children and take the boys to the local library on a regular basis. The younger boy is the same age as your son so I have a good idea of the types of activities that a three-year-old might enjoy. As well as taking the older boy to school, I take the younger boy to nursery class.

I also have experience of working with three- to five-year-olds in a nursery/reception unit at a primary school. Although I liked the challenge involved in working with young children in a classroom setting, I decided that I would prefer working as a nanny. I feel that my quiet but enthusiastic approach to early learning is more suited to caring for children on a one-to-one basis. I enjoy the chance to give children the individual attention and understanding that is more possible when working as a nanny.

I have been told how evident it is that I like children. I feel that I do have a good rapport with young children. I believe that by providing the encouragement and support they need in a warm, friendly and enthusiastic way, any young child in my care will be able to achieve their own individual potential.

I hope that you will consider my application carefully. I think that I could provide excellent care for your son. At 26 years old, I am reliable and competent as well as being prepared to devote my full attention to the responsibilities of looking after a young child. (As one of my current employers is a veterinary surgeon and the other is a doctor I have to be both flexible and reliable.)

I enclose my curriculum vitae giving full details of my qualifications and experience. I look forward to hearing from you soon.

Yours sincerely,

EXERCISE: Select one of the advertisements for a nanny job that you found earlier. Write a letter in reply to the advertisement, highlighting why you are interested in the job and giving details of your qualifications and/or relevant experience.

Preparing your curriculum vitae

A curriculum vitae (CV) is a summary of your employment history. Your CV can be copied and used each time you make a job application. To create a positive impression for future employers, make sure your CV:

* is neat, legible and clearly presented
* is typed or word-processed so that it may be faxed and photocopied
* has a maximum of two pages
* is up-to-date, by adding any new jobs and references
* is factual, positive and concise
* includes all your qualifications
* includes any relevant practical work.

EXERCISE: Prepare (or update) your curriculum vitae.

REFERENCES

As there are currently no legal requirements on a person applying for a job as a nanny, the employer must be confident as far as possible that they are making the right decision about employing you. You should expect all prospective employers to check your identity, background, qualifications and employment history. At an interview you will be asked for proof of identity and at least two references.

Proof of identity

You can use your birth certificate, passport or full driving licence as proof of your identity. Agencies and/or employers will need to see the originals as photocopying can disguise forgeries. At least one of these forms of identity must carry a photograph.

References

Employers will usually ask you for at least two references, even if you are from a nanny agency. One reference should be from your current or last employer. If you are a student straight from college, you should supply a reference from your college tutor and another reference from your final work placement. Ask permission from the person before you give their details as a referee.

A potential employer will contact your referees and ask them about:

❋ your work when they employed you as a nanny/nursery nurse

❋ how they rated your care of the children

❋ why you left their employment

❋ what your strengths and weaknesses were

❋ any difficulties they think you might have if you were left in sole charge of a child

❋ any health problems and sick leave you had during your employment

❋ whether they would consider re-employing you.

(DfES 2004)

YOUR PROFESSIONAL PORTFOLIO

You should prepare and organize a professional portfolio. If you prepare a well-presented professional portfolio in advance, with all the relevant documents that will be required when you are invited for an interview, it will save time when you apply for jobs or register with a nanny agency. Having a well-presented portfolio will demonstrate to potential employers that you are well organized and have a professional attitude towards your career as a nanny.

Your professional portfolio may include:

* school examination certificates
* college certificate or diploma
* first aid certificate
* basic food hygiene certificate
* curriculum vitae
* written references
* statement of your childcare philosophy
* examples of previous work with children
* relevant college assignments
* Enhanced Disclosure from the Criminal Records bureau (if you have one).

You can use a display or presentation album with plastic pockets to organize your portfolio. Your portfolio should include the originals of your school examination certificates and college certificate or diploma. Make sure that your first aid certificate is up-to-date.

Your curriculum vitae and references should also be updated as you gain more work experience and/or further qualifications. You could also include examples of previous work with young children or relevant college assignments, e.g. activity plans suitable for a young child in the home or working with parents in a family setting.

> **EXERCISE:** Compile a professional portfolio if you do not have one already.

PREPARING FOR INTERVIEWS

When you succeed in getting an interview do not waste the opportunity. The employer is interested in your skills, qualifications and potential commitment to the job. The interview is an opportunity for the employer to test your suitability for the job in relation to other people who are also being interviewed. The interview is also your chance to meet the potential employer and to find out more about the job. Look at an interview as an opportunity for an exchange of information.

Find out as much as you can about the job beforehand. Refresh your memory by looking at the advertisement again, any information about the post from the agency or notes you have made after talking to the parent on the telephone. Think about the following:

* What are the main duties and responsibilities of the job?
* What qualities and skills can you offer?

* Have you got the necessary qualifications and/or experience?
* Why are you applying?
* Are you clear about the family's needs?
* How will you present this information at the interview?

It can be helpful and build confidence to rehearse or practise mock interviews. Remember this is the point where you will be competing against other people who have also been selected for an interview for this particular job. The way you present yourself at the interview is very important.

Personal appearance

Dress professionally and appropriately for the interview by wearing something smart but comfortable. A suit is probably a little too formal – after all, you want to appear friendly and approachable to both the parents and the children. A smart, casual dress (or casual shirt and trousers) with a tailored jacket is ideal. Wear sensible shoes – no high heels. Keep any jewellery to a minimum; avoid dangling earrings, loads of rings and bangles. Make sure your overall appearance is clean and tidy, including fingernails, which should be kept short, especially if the post involves caring for a baby or a very young child. Make sure your hair is well groomed; keep long hair tied back and avoid outrageous hairstyles – a Mohican is not likely to inspire the employer's confidence in your childcare abilities!

Body language

Look alert and interested. Do not yawn or look bored. Do not sit or stand with your arms folded. Smile, look relaxed and shake hands. Look at the interviewer and show an interest in what is being said

What to do and say at interviews to get the job you want

Arrive in plenty of time for the interview; not only is it courteous, but it also demonstrates that you are punctual – an essential quality for a reliable and professional nanny. Remember these important points:

1 The first two or three minutes of an interview are important for creating a good first impression. Try to develop a friendly approach and address the person by name.

2 Listen carefully to each question. Take a moment to think about the question before answering. Speak clearly and not too quickly.

3 Avoid using slang or unprofessional speech, e.g. always say 'children', not 'kids'.

4 Be natural and honest. Do not claim to have more knowledge and experience than you really do. Be positive and concentrate on the achievements and relevant experience that you do have.

5 Do not answer questions with just a 'yes' or 'no'; use examples and give reasons for your opinions, but remember to stick to the point.

6 Show enthusiasm, but do not be aggressive or pushy.

7 Be ready to ask questions. Make sure you have prepared some questions to ask before the interview.

8 If you have the opportunity to meet the child or children, make sure you pay particular attention to them.

9 Discuss salary at the end of the interview unless it is mentioned earlier.

10 Ask how long you are likely to wait for a decision.

EXERCISE: Make a list of questions you might like to ask at an interview.

QUESTIONS YOU MIGHT BE ASKED AT INTERVIEW

It is a good idea to think about how you will answer the sorts of questions that parents (or agencies) might ask you at an interview for a job as a nanny. Here are some questions you might be asked at interview:

* How long have you been a nanny?

* What ages of children have you worked with?

* Why do you enjoy working with children?

* What do you think are your particular strengths when working with children?

* What childcare training and qualifications do you have?

* What special skills or creative talents do you have? (e.g. cooking, arts and crafts, playing a musical instrument)

* Which aspects of this particular job do you think you will enjoy?

* How might you spend the day with a baby or young child?

* What difficulties have you experienced as a nanny and how were they resolved?

* What would you do if a child had an accident while in your care?

* How would you deal with a young child's difficult behaviour, e.g. a temper tantrum?

* How many days have you had off sick in the last 12 months?

* Why did you leave your last job or why will you be leaving your present position?

(DfES 2004)

IMPORTANT ISSUES TO DISCUSS AT INTERVIEW

The interview should be a two-way process. You should be offered the chance to ask your own questions. Make sure that you discuss these important issues if they have not already been raised in the interview:

* the salary details, including tax and National Insurance arrangements
* how payment will be made, e.g. weekly or monthly, by cheque or directly into a bank account
* the hours and exact duties of the job (including how much housework you would be expected to do and how many hours of babysitting)
* any particular house rules, especially if it is a live-in position
* when you would be expected to start if offered the job
* holiday entitlements
* length of probationary period
* positive discipline strategies – a childcare professional never uses physical punishment as a form of discipline (be sure that you and the parents are in agreement about discipline)
* child safety: in the home and garden (including dealing with pets); on public transport or in the car; on outings.

(DfES 2004)

EXERCISE: Consider any other important issues you might like to discuss at an interview.

AFTER THE INTERVIEW

While it is fresh in your mind, think about how the interview went and make a note of any points for which you were not prepared or questions you found difficult to answer.

Applying for jobs is almost a full time job in itself! You will need to organize your job applications in a business-like way. Establish your own record and filing system (e.g. a separate document wallet for each job or agency application) so that you can:

* make a note of which jobs and/or agencies you have applied for (with dates)
* keep job advertisements or agency information

* store copies of your application forms and/or covering letters
* list further developments, e.g. second interviews
* store any correspondence, e.g. rejection letters and job offers.

EXERCISE: Organize your job applications. Establish your own record and filing system for these.

What to do if you do not get the job

If you are unsuccessful after a job interview you may feel some anxiety or even depression, especially if you are finding it difficult to get a job. How you handle rejection will depend on:

* your own expectations of how easy or difficult it is to get a job
* how much effort and planning you put in
* your anticipation of any possible difficulties
* your personality, e.g. whether you tend to be pessimistic or optimistic
* other areas of stress in your life, e.g. worries about money, relationships.

If you are feeling anxious, depressed or resentful about not getting a particular job, you should talk to your family or close friends about it. They should be able to help you keep things in perspective – just because you did not get this job does not mean you will never get a job.

Try to learn from the experience and take positive action towards being more successful next time:

* build on your experience with each interview so that you become more confident and knowledgeable
* be positive by focusing on your achievements so far
* identify and improve on any problem areas, e.g. developing better communication skills
* improve your interview technique by practising with a friend
* consider studying for (additional) qualifications
* if you are currently unemployed, consider doing voluntary work to gain more experience.

Remember that there are more parents wishing to employ a professional nanny than there are nannies looking for employment. Try not to take rejection too personally. The other applicants may have had better qualifications or more experience. Keep trying! You *will* get the nanny job that is just right for you and your particular skills.

What to do if you are offered the job

When you receive an offer, respond as quickly as possible. Usually you will have your answer ready. If you need time to make up your mind finally (or if you are waiting for the results of other interviews), you should ask the employer if you may have until a given date before sending a firm reply. If you are not sure, you could ask for a second interview where you could meet other members of the family and spend a little more time with the child or children.

Even if you feel it might be the perfect job for you, do not make a hasty decision. Take your time to consider whether you would feel happy with the family and their routines. If there are areas that you feel could lead to potential problems or serious conflicts (e.g. you do not agree with the parents' views on discipline), you should not take the job. If you decide to accept the job, do not hand in your notice until you have received written confirmation that you have got the job.

Further reading

Amos, J., 2003, *Writing a Winning CV: essential CV writing skills that will get you the job you want*, How To Books.

Hobart, C. and Frankel, J., 1996, *Practical Guide to Childcare Employment*, Nelson Thornes.

Hobart, C. and Frankel, J., 2001, *Nannying: a guide to good practice*, Nelson Thornes.

Parkinson, M., 2002, *Your Job Search Made Easy: everything you need to know about applications, interviews and tests*, Kogan Page.

 The contract of employment

 The job description

 Statutory employment rights

 Salaries

 Insurance

 Getting a disclosure

THE CONTRACT OF EMPLOYMENT

Legal requirements

By law, most employees who are employed for a month or more must receive a written statement of employment within eight weeks of starting employment. The written statement or contract of employment must include: the start date, the period of employment and notice, main duties, working hours, salary, holidays, sick pay and grounds for dismissal.

If you have agreed to be employed by two families as part of a nanny-share, you will need a separate written statement or contract of employment between you and each family so that everyone is clear about your hours and exact duties for each family.

Contents of the contract

As well as what is required by law, it is helpful for a nanny to have a written contract of employment that also includes more detailed information so that you and your employers are both clear about what you expect from each other. You should make sure the contract of employment covers all aspects regarding your care of the child or children and your conduct in the family home.

Although the law says you must have a contract within eight weeks of employment, ideally you should ask for a written contract after you accept an offer of employment and before you start work.

To avoid misunderstandings and possible problems, make sure your contract of employment includes the following:

* name and address of your employer
* your name and address
* your hours of work
* a job description with your exact duties in detail
* how many nights' babysitting will be required
* your salary and salary review
* extra pay (or time off in lieu) for extra hours in emergencies or on bank holidays
* holiday and sick pay entitlements
* notice periods
* use of the telephone
* a description of your accommodation if you are living in
* who pays the bills concerning your accommodation
* if a car is provided, who pays the insurance
* if you use your own car, who pays expenses when you are using it for work
* who pays the extra insurance premium for using your car at work.

Most problems experienced by a nanny when starting a new job involve a mismatch between the actual duties and those the nanny agreed with the employer at interview. For example, you may find that the salary is less than you had expected it to be or that you are expected to do extra household chores and cooking duties.

A sample contract of employment for a nanny is set out below:

Details of employment

Name and address of employer: ....

Name and address of employee: ....

Date of issue of this contract: ....

Date of commencement: .... Expiry date (if known): ....

Place of employment: ....

Job title: ....

Payment terms

The Employee will receive £................ gross per annum/week (which is £............. net per week), payable calendar monthly/weekly in arrears. The Employer is responsible for paying the Employee's tax and National Insurance. The salary will be reviewed after .... and also if a nanny-share scheme comes into operation.

Hours of work

The hours of work will be .... for .... days per week. These hours of work can only be changed by mutual agreement (include any evening/weekend babysitting agreements).

Duties

The Employee will be responsible for normal nursery duties as stated in the job description (if there is no job description, be sure to state clearly here exactly what duties are expected).

Expenses

The Employer will reimburse all reasonable expenses incurred in the course of duties in caring for the children. This includes: outings (see safety); the Employee's midday meal and all soft drinks, tea and coffee consumed by the Employee; entertaining other children and carers (within reason); and purchases on behalf of the children, with the prior agreement of the Employer.

General

(State clearly any agreement regarding the use of the car, rules about smoking, socializing, telephone calls and use of the house facilities.)

Days off

The Employee is entitled to .... days off each week (state arrangements for weekends).

Holidays

The Employee will be allowed four weeks' (20 working days) paid holiday each year to be taken at times agreed between the Employee and the Employer. In the first and final years of service the Employee will be entitled to holidays on a pro-rata basis (paid compensation is not normally given for holidays not actually taken). Holidays may only be carried into the next year with the permission of the Employer. The Employee will be free on all bank holidays, or will receive a day off in lieu by agreement.

Other paid employment

The Employee may take on other paid work only with the agreement of the Employer. In any event of a nanny-share being suggested, it is a condition of employment that the main income of such a nanny-share will be the Employer's and the Employee will receive an increase in his/her remuneration, to be agreed between all parties.

Sickness

In general the Employer will allow five working days' sickness at full pay in one year. After the fourth working day of sickness, SSP would apply at £............... per day.

Safety

The Employer must be kept informed at all times, where possible, of the children's whereabouts, and must know and approve of any other people the children meet on a regular basis. Similarly, they must be kept informed in advance of people invited to visit the Employer's residence.

Termination

The first .... weeks/months of employment will be probationary. During the probationary period, either the Employee or the Employer may terminate the employment by giving one week's notice in writing. Following the probationary period, either party may terminate this contract by giving .... weeks'/months' notice.

Confidentiality

It is a condition of employment that now, and at all times in the future, the Employee maintains the strictest confidence concerning the Employer, family and all business concerns.

Pensions

There is no pension scheme applicable to this employment.

Grievances

If the Employee has any grievances against the Employer, these should be discussed only with the Employer and not disclosed to any other parties.

Disciplinary Procedures

Reasons that might give rise to the need to take disciplinary action include the following:

1   causing a disruptive influence
2   incompetence
3   unsatisfactory standard of dress or appearance
4   conduct during or outside working hours that may prove prejudicial to the interests or reputation of the Employer
5   unreliable timekeeping or attendance
6   failure to comply with agreed instructions/procedures
7   rudeness or lack of consideration
8   breach of confidentiality
9   serious cases may result in instant dismissal, but the usual procedure will be:
    a. verbal warning
    b. written warning
    c. dismissal

Gross misconduct, which could result in instant dismissal, includes the following:

10   violent or abusive behaviour
11   any action that could endanger or cause harm to children in the Employee's care
12   drunkenness or use of illegal drugs.

Signed by the Employer   Signed by the Employee

Signature ....   Signature ....

Date ....   Date ....

A probationary period

Once you have accepted a job as a nanny you should agree a probationary period. A probationary period will allow you and the family to try out arrangements before you both commit yourselves to a more permanent agreement. You should ensure that any agreed probationary period is clearly stated in your contract of employment and includes the period of notice required during this period. For example, a probationary period of four weeks or one month is quite usual, with either party being able to terminate the employment by giving one week's notice in writing.

THE JOB DESCRIPTION

In addition to your contract, it is very helpful for you and your employer to draw up a job description specifying your exact duties and responsibilities, which could include information on: managing petty cash, security of the home, answering the telephone, communication with the parents (including keeping records), activities at home, hygiene, rest periods, play and exercise, household duties (e.g. clothes, bedding, cleaning, meals), safety (e.g. house, garden, car, outings), managing children's behaviour, playgroup/nursery/school arrangements, leisure activities, birthday parties, health screening (e.g. clinics, routine checks, dentist). A sample job description is set out below:

General duties

❋ Ensuring without prompting that there are sufficient supplies of stock items such as bread, cereal, milk, washing powder and nappies, for each day, including weekends.

❋ Doing daily shopping and preparing food for the children as necessary; your shopping load should not be excessive and should be able to be carried easily by hand or on a baby buggy. (Your employers should do the main shop.)

❋ Keep an account of all money spent on items for the children and on meals for yourself and the children's friends so expenses can be calculated; where possible, obtain receipts.

❋ The employer may provide a float and should be given at least one day's notice when this needs replacing or when extra funds are required for agreed outings, presents etc.

❋ Keep a note or diary of the day's events for each child in your care (for the parents).

❋ Organizing birthday parties for the children.

❋ Buying small birthday presents and cards for other children and wrapping them if the children go to a party.

❋ Running small errands, such as returning videotapes and library books on time, buying stamps, taking shoes for repair, collecting dry cleaning etc.

❋ Securing the house and ensuring that all windows and doors are locked whenever the house is left, even for short periods of time.

Childcare

Daily care of the children with sole charge Monday to Friday from ....
a.m. to .... p.m. Babysitting and weekend arrangements should be clearly
stated for a live-in nanny.

To include:

* Preparing, serving and clearing away breakfast, lunch and tea for the
  children, and/or sterilizing and preparing baby feeds.
* Preparing packed lunches for the children to take to school.
* Taking the children to school/nursery and picking them up punctually at
  the agreed times.
* Ensuring the children have appropriate clean clothes each day, including
  sportswear.
* Taking the children to clubs and/or activities each week.
* Ensuring that the children meet up with other children/friends in both
  their home and at other children's homes during the week.
* Taking the children to the local health centre for check-ups and
  vaccinations by arrangement, and to the dentist when necessary.
* Liaison with staff at school, attending any meetings held in connection
  with the school, checking that messages from the school such as details of
  outings etc. are passed on and informing your employers of any meetings
  or areas of concern.
* You may also want to clarify the amount of time the child is allowed to
  spend watching TV, videos etc., and how much time can be spent playing
  with other children.
* You should also add something about emergency routines for contacting
  parents, and in what situation they are to be contacted, e.g. for earache or
  a bump on the head.

Household duties

Carefully agree these so there is no misunderstanding later on. To include:

* Washing, ironing and putting away the children's clothes, ensuring there
  is a sufficient supply of clean clothes for the weekend and checking
  clothes and toys at regular intervals for damage and putting aside any that
  have been outgrown.
* Doing the children's or general washing by machine, when the load is
  large enough, hanging it out to dry or tumble-drying.
* Doing daily washing up, by machine if there is a large enough load,
  putting it all away.
* General tidying of living room, kitchen and children's rooms each day, also
  bathroom and toilet if used for children's care. For live-in nannies include
  the nanny's room and bathroom and tidying up after yourself in the house.
* Answering the telephone, taking and relaying messages.
* Being available to take deliveries, give access to workmen etc., by
  arrangement.

Sample job description (reproduced by kind permission of Toybox Nanny Agency tel. 01883 722322)

STATUTORY EMPLOYMENT RIGHTS

In addition to the written statement of employment, as a nanny you are also entitled to a number of statutory employment rights that apply to all employees as soon as they start work. These include protection against:

❋ unlawful deductions from your salary

❋ adverse treatment on grounds of your sex, race or disability

❋ dismissal for seeking to enforce your statutory employment rights.

Other statutory employment rights that apply to working as a nanny include:

❋ Maximum working hours: as a nanny you are covered by the Working Time Directive, which regulates the hours an employee can be expected to work. Your employer cannot insist that you work more than 48 hours per week. However, you could agree to work longer hours by both signing a written agreement, which can be cancelled at any time, with an agreed period of notice.

❋ National Minimum Wage: your employer must pay you at least £4.10 per hour if you are aged 18–21 years, and £4.85 per hour if you are aged 22 or over (from 1 October 2004). However, your employer may not have to pay you the minimum wage if you are living as part of their household.

❋ Statutory Sick Pay (SSP): your employer must pay you SSP if you are sick for four days or more.

❋ Paid annual holiday: as an employee, whether full-time or part-time, you are entitled to four weeks' annual paid leave. You should be able to negotiate the holiday periods with your employer.

❋ Notice of termination of employment: as a nanny you are entitled to one week's notice if your employer terminates your employment when you have been working for more than one month. When your employer has employed you for two years, you are entitled to two weeks' notice. This continues (one week for each year worked) until you have worked for the same employer for 12 years. The notice period can be overridden by a longer period if it is included in your contract of employment. For example, it is usual practice to give four weeks' notice (after the probationary period), as this gives the family time to make alternative childcare arrangements.

Other statutory employment rights apply on completion of a qualifying period of service. For example:

❋ Protection against unfair dismissal: if you have been in continuous employment (with the same employer) for at least one year you are automatically protected against unfair dismissal.

❋ Statutory Maternity Pay (SMP): if you become pregnant and have been working for the same employer for at least nine months prior to the baby's due date, you are entitled to SMP and maternity leave.

* Statutory Paternity Pay (SPP): as of April 2003 new fathers are entitled to two weeks' SPP, with a right to a further 13 weeks of unpaid leave. To qualify, you must have been in continuous employment for at least six months.

* Redundancy pay: you are entitled to redundancy pay if you have been in continuous employment for a minimum of two years, as long as you are not employed on a fixed-term contract.

SALARIES

Beyond the legal requirement to be paid the National Minimum Wage, there are no fixed rules concerning the level of pay for a nanny. However, there are several factors that you can reasonably expect will affect the salary. The salary you can expect to receive will depend on:

1   The location of the position. If you work in London, you can expect salary levels to be higher as they are subject to the same weighting as other professions. You can also expect pay levels to be higher in areas where a large number of parents are competing for a small number of nannies.

2   Whether the position is live-in or live-out. As a live-in nanny you can expect to be paid less than a daily (live-out) nanny. However, even though you earn less money, this is compensated for by the additional benefits that you would receive as a live-in nanny, such as free accommodation and food.

3   Your age, experience and/or qualifications. If you are a recently qualified and/or inexperienced nanny you should expect to earn less than a nanny with two or more years' experience (whether qualified or unqualified). If you have lots of childcare experience and excellent references or you are a Norland, Chiltern or Montessori trained nanny, then you can expect to earn a higher salary. Experience of caring for children with special needs can also increase your salary.

These were the average salaries for nannies in 2003:

Daily (live-out) nanny	Annual gross	Weekly net
Central London	£27,320	£384
Outer London/South-east	£22,120	£319
Other cities and towns	£18,786	£276
Rural areas	£18,546	£273
Live-in nanny	Annual gross	Weekly net
Central London	£21,343	£308
Outer London/South-east	£17,458	£257
Other cities and towns	£15,521	£234
Rural areas	£15,450	£233

Professional Nanny Supplement in *Nursery World*, January 2004

TAX AND NATIONAL INSURANCE

All nannies (except maternity nurses and some temporary nannies) are employed, rather than self-employed, which means that your employer is responsible for paying your tax and National Insurance contributions. Many nannies agree their salaries on the basis of a net figure, which is the amount of money after all deductions have been taken off. If this is the case, your employer will have to pay your tax and National Insurance contributions on top of the agreed net figure.

If you agree a gross wage, then deductions will come out of that amount. It is better for you to agree a gross wage, as you will then receive the benefit of any government increases in the personal tax allowance and any cuts in income tax rates. A gross wage also allows you to compare your salary with other childcare professionals.

Agreeing a gross wage is also better for your employer; otherwise they end up paying your tax and National Insurance contributions without taking into account your personal tax position and regardless of any changes in legislation. This could mean your employer's actual cost of employing you could be as much as 50 per cent more than your agreed net pay (Nilsdotter, *Early Years Educator*, November 2003).

Your employer is required by law to register with the Inland Revenue under the PAYE scheme and must declare your employment to them. Your employer must pay accurate tax and National Insurance contributions to the Inland Revenue on a monthly or quarterly basis. Your employer must give you a payslip listing your earnings, including all the tax and National Insurance deductions that have been made. If your employer does not want to manage your PAYE, they can use a specialist nanny payroll firm or get their accountant to do it.

In the past, some employers have failed to pay some or all of their nannies' income tax due to the Inland Revenue. As from 1 January 2001, if an employer pays their employee cash in hand without paying the proper tax to the Inland Revenue they are committing a criminal offence and are liable to fines of up to £5,000.

EXERCISE: Find out about the salaries for nannies in your local area. You could check with local nanny agencies, local colleges offering childcare courses and in local newspaper advertisements.

INSURANCE

There are three types of insurance that are relevant to your employment as a nanny:

* public and employer's liability insurance
* car insurance
* professional indemnity insurance.

Public and employer's liability insurance

Check that your employer has public liability insurance to cover personal injury if you have an accident in their home.

Car insurance

If you drive your employer's car, you should check that you are included on their car insurance policy. If you use your own car to transport the children, you will need car insurance for business use. This is more expensive, so make sure you agree with your employer how the extra premiums will be paid, e.g. your employer could pay the difference between your usual car insurance cover and the business car insurance.

Professional indemnity insurance

It is also a good idea to take out professional indemnity insurance (or nanny insurance) to provide you with cover in case a child suffers a serious injury while in your care.

GETTING A DISCLOSURE

The term 'police check' is now obsolete in the UK. Although many people still use this term, the correct terminology is actually 'disclosure'.

The Criminal Records Bureau

The Police Act 1997 (Part V) was introduced to protect certain vulnerable groups. The Act makes applicants for certain posts 'exempt' from declining to give employers details of their past criminal history. These posts include those involving access to children, young people, the elderly, disabled people, alcohol or drug users and the chronically sick. Organizations that include exempt posts are legally entitled to ask applicants for details of all convictions, whether they are 'spent' or 'unspent' under the Rehabilitation of Offenders Act 1974. Registered organizations are now authorized to obtain details of an applicant's criminal history from the Criminal Records Bureau (CRB), an executive agency of the Home Office. The details of this information are set out in a disclosure.

There are three types of disclosure: Basic, Standard and Enhanced.

1   Basic Disclosures: these are not suitable for applicants intending to work with children, the elderly and other vulnerable groups. A Basic Disclosure only includes information held on central police records that are unspent according to the Rehabilitation of Offenders Act 1974.

2   Standard Disclosures: these include information about spent, unspent convictions, cautions, warnings and reprimands. Standard Disclosures are available for applicants applying for posts involving regular contact with children and/or other vulnerable groups. A Standard Disclosure also checks information held by the Department of Health and Department for Education and Skills (List 99). A Standard Disclosure can only be obtained through a Registered Body to the CRB and not by the individuals themselves.

3   Enhanced Disclosures: these are for posts listed in Section 115 of The Police Act 1997, such as those involving unsupervised contact with children, young people and vulnerable groups. It is the most comprehensive and appropriate check that is available to organizations and gives thorough information on all records held:

    ❊   the police national computer for convictions
    ❊   the Department of Health and Department for Education and Skills (List 99)
    ❊   the POCA list (Protection of Children Act)
    ❊   the POVA list (Protection of Vulnerable Adults).

    These are lists of adults who are considered not suitable to work with children, but who may not have been prosecuted. The Chief Officer of Police may also release information for inclusion in an Enhanced Disclosure and additional information may be sent which is not released to the applicant. An Enhanced Disclosure can only be obtained through a Registered Body to the CRB and not by the individuals themselves.

Why do you need an Enhanced Disclosure?

If you are seeking employment as a nanny without using a nanny agency, at the moment there is no legal requirement for you to obtain a disclosure. However, it would be beneficial for you to register with an agency in order to obtain a disclosure. An Enhanced Disclosure is the type of disclosure most suitable for employment as a nanny because you will have unsupervised contact with young children.

   If you are seeking employment via a nanny agency, it is a legal requirement for the agency to obtain a disclosure on your behalf. The Protection of Children Act 1999 and the Criminal Justice and Court Services Act 2000 make it an offence for any organization to offer employment involving regular contact with children to anyone who has been convicted of certain offences or included on lists of people considered unsuitable for such work. The Act applies to employment agencies, including nanny agencies.

The Department for Education and Skills has set out guidelines for nanny agencies, including interviewing prospective nannies and carrying out the relevant qualification and background checks to ensure they are properly qualified to work with children. A nanny agency will apply for an Enhanced Disclosure on your behalf via an umbrella organization registered with the CRB. You will receive a copy of your Enhanced Disclosure. The agency may charge you about £40–50 for this service.

With an Enhanced Disclosure you can prove to a potential employer at the interview stage that you have no criminal convictions that could potentially put a child at risk. An Enhanced Disclosure will also demonstrate to prospective employers that you are serious about your career as a childcare professional.

EXERCISE: If you do not have an Enhanced Disclosure, register with a local nanny agency to get one as soon as possible.

Further reading

Department of Health, Home Office and Department for Education and Employment, 1999, *Working Together to Safeguard Children*, HMSO.

Department of Trade and Industry (DTI), August 2001, *Contracts of Employment* (PL810 Rev 6) and August 2000, *Written Statements of Employment Practice* (PL700 Rev 5); two free booklets that may help in drafting a nanny's contract (both are available from your local Jobcentre or the DTI website: www.dti.gov.uk).

Department of Trade and Industry (DTI), July 2003, *A Guide to Working Time Regulations*; a free booklet available from the DTI or the DTI website (see above).

Department of Trade and Industry (DTI), July 2003, *Individual Rights of Employees* (PL716 Rev 10) and May 2003, *Redundancy Entitlement – Statutory Rights* (PL808 Rev 6); booklets can be obtained from your local Jobcentre or the DTI website (see above).

Professional Association of Nursery Nurses (PANN), 2002, *All You Need to Know About Working as a Nanny*; a booklet containing information about qualifications, agencies, interviews, duties a nanny is usually expected to undertake, advice on current pay scales and insurance issues and a sample contract of employment (the booklet is available for a small charge).

 Transitions

 Preparing for and coping with transitions

 Settling in

 Managing your time

 The probationary period

TRANSITIONS

The first few weeks with a new family involve a period of 'getting to know you'. You need to get to know the children and their parents, and they all need to get to know you. During the early days of working in a new nanny position you need to ensure that the transition runs as smoothly as possible for everyone involved.

To do this effectively you need to know and understand:

✳ what transitions mean for young children

✳ how to prepare young children for transitions

✳ how to help young children cope with the transition

✳ the importance of sharing information with the parents

✳ how to find your way around the family home

✳ how to find your way around the local area

✳ a range of settling-in strategies

✳ how to manage your time effectively.

What do transitions involve?

Transitions involve young children dealing with changes from one care and education setting to another, or a change from one carer to another. Here are some examples:

✳ from parent to nanny working in the child's own home

✳ from one nanny to a different nanny

* from home to playgroup, nursery or school
* from home to childminder's home
* from playgroup or nursery to school
* from the Foundation Stage to Key Stage 1 (infants)
* from Key Stage 1 (infants) to Key Stage 2 (juniors)
* from primary school to secondary school.

Transitions can also involve other significant changes in the child's life, such as:

* death or serious illness of a family member or close friend
* parental separation or divorce
* moving to a different area, county or country
* moving house
* going into hospital
* death of a favourite pet
* arrival of a new baby or stepbrothers and sisters
* going on holiday (especially visiting another country).

To cope with the change, separation and loss involved in transitions, young children need:

* help to prepare for such transitions
* help to accept transitions and settle into new settings or with new carers
* reassurance from adults to maintain their feelings of stability, security and trust
* adult assistance to adjust to different social rules and social expectations
* help in adapting to group situations.

PREPARING FOR AND COPING WITH TRANSITIONS

Young children's responses to transitions often depend on the way they are prepared for the new carer, setting or situation. The need for preparation was not recognized in the past (e.g. young children started school or went into hospital and were left to cope with the situation with little or no preparation beforehand, and parental involvement was positively discouraged).

EXERCISE: Think about your first day at school. What was it like? How were you prepared for this new situation?

Many young children experience anxiety and stress when they first have a new carer or attend a new setting, due to:

* separation from their parent or previous carer
* encountering unfamiliar children who may have established friendships already
* the length of time spent in the setting, e.g. 8 a.m. to 6 p.m. in a day nursery or 9 a.m. to 3.30 p.m. in school
* differences in culture and language of the setting to child's previous experiences
* unfamiliar routines and rules
* worry about doing the wrong thing
* unfamiliar activities, such as PE, playtime, lunchtime or even story-time
* the unfamiliar physical environment, which may seem overwhelming and scary
* difficulties in following more structured activities and adult directions
* concentrating on activities for longer than previously used to.

To alleviate some of this anxiety and stress, preparation is now seen as an essential part of successful transitions, which may include nannies, childminders, nurseries, schools, foster care and hospitals. Most settings have established procedures for preparing children for transitions.

Preparing babies and young children for transitions

* In the first week arrange for one of the child's parents to stay at home before you have sole charge of the child (see below).
* You and/or the parents should talk to the child about what is going to happen.
* Obtain detailed information from the parents so that the child's individual needs can be identified (this includes the baby's or child's existing daily routine, eating and sleeping patterns, special dietary requirements, the child's likes and dislikes regarding food, clothes, toys and activities).
* Ensure you have the parents' contact details in case of emergencies as well as any medical information regarding the child, e.g. allergies, asthma, eczema.
* Provide parents with information about how you will help the child to settle in.
* Plan appropriate activities for the first few days/weeks that provide reassurance to both child and parents.
* Make sure the child has easy access to a particular comfort object or favourite toy if they have one.

Transition objects

A transition object is a comfort object that a baby or young child uses to provide reassurance and security when separated from a parent. The child feels connected to the parent by holding, cuddling, stroking or sucking the object. Transition objects are usually something soft like a small blanket, muslin cloth or cuddly toy such as a teddy bear.

Young child with a transition object

Transition objects provide a link between the young child and the absent parent that enables the child to feel more secure in new situations without the parent or with a new carer. Reliance on a comfort object does not mean the child is insecure or too dependent on the parent. It may actually enable the child to become more independent and secure as they have the object to reassure them in the parent's absence. A young child without a comfort object may not have this reassurance or feeling of security.

Some young children have their comfort object with them at all times; some just at bedtime, during naps or to relax with when they need a break; others only when entering new situations, such as visiting the GP, clinic or hospital, or starting nursery or playgroup.

A strong attachment to a comfort object usually begins in a child's first year and often increases between the ages of one and two years. By the time a child is three or four years old the need for their comfort object usually lessens. Many children are less attached to their comfort object by the time they start school. A child may continue to need their comfort object for the occasional snuggle when they are very tired or distressed until they are teenagers. There is no set age for giving up a comfort object.

Bottles should not be used as comfort objects because they are unhygienic (e.g. bacteria in milk kept around too long), prolonged contact with teeth can lead to dental decay and can contribute to problems with the child's bite.

Dummies can be acceptable as comfort objects if well kept (they are no less hygienic than thumb sucking), but you should discourage prolonged use as this can restrict the child's communication. Comfort habits include thumb sucking and twiddling/sucking hair. These can be difficult to stop as the comfort 'object' is with the child forever!

One of your first priorities is to meet the individual needs of the child, so if the child feels more emotionally secure, reassured and relaxed due to the presence of a comfort object, you should accommodate it. Attitudes towards transition/comfort objects or habits vary between individuals, so discuss the parents' wishes regarding the child's comfort object.

Remember these important points:

* Allow a baby or young child to have free access to their comfort object at all times as this can assist their sense of security, especially during transitional periods.

* Separation from a comfort object (e.g. in order to participate in messy activities or mealtimes) must be done gently; it is the most precious thing the child has.

* Comfort objects are usually irreplaceable, so check with parents that a replacement or substitute is available if the worst happens.

* Let the child decide when a comfort object is no longer necessary.

* An older child may need access to a comfort object while experiencing exceptional distress on separating from parents or where other factors make this necessary (e.g. special needs such as emotional or behavioural difficulties).

* With an older child (as their confidence in being with you increases), set time limits as to when they can have their comfort object (e.g. they can have it at bedtime or when they are ill, distressed or have an accident).

* Anything that makes transitions easier for young children (such as comfort objects) should be regarded in a positive way .

SETTLING IN

You should make sure you know a range of strategies to make things easier for everyone during the settling-in period, including creating a positive first impression, sharing information with the parents, maintaining the child's usual routines, making arrangements for the first week and planning activities to help the child cope with a change in carer.

Positive first impressions

You can expect to feel a bit shy and awkward at first, but remember the child will also be feeling this way. If a child is withdrawn to begin with, do not worry too much as they will soon adjust to your arrival.

The first thing a child needs to know is that they will be safe both physically and emotionally when they are with you. Remember that all children have different levels of emotional security; some may be quite confident and outgoing from the outset, while others may be shy and wary at first.

When you first meet the child be sure to smile and make eye contact. Say hello in a warm, friendly manner, using the child's preferred name (e.g. a boy named Thomas may prefer to be called Tom, or a girl named Christine may prefer to be called Chris). Eye contact is very important because it helps to create a personal relationship between you and the child.

Young children can tell if you are genuinely interested in them and the job of looking after them. Remember you only get one chance to make a first impression, so make sure you make a positive first impression with the child. For example, you could pay the child a sincere compliment, such as, 'What a lovely dress/fantastic t-shirt you are wearing!' You could tell the child a fun story or an amazing fact. Bring something interesting or unusual with you to stimulate the child's curiosity (e.g. a cuddly toy, clever pop-up book or magic trick, depending on the age of the child). If you are friendly and positive, the child will start to feel that being with you will be a fun and positive experience.

Create a positive atmosphere right from the start. Ask the child about their favourite things and share information about yourself as well. Remember that getting to know each other is a two-way process.

Ten ways to create a positive first impression

You can get your relationship with the family off to a good start by:

1 Planning appropriate activities for the first few days/weeks that provide reassurance to both the child and the parents.

2 Providing opportunities for imaginative play to let the child express any feelings and fears about the transition.

3 Listening to the child and providing reassurance that everything will be fine.

4 Being flexible and adaptable concerning the family's routines.

5 Keeping to the child's usual daily routine.

6 Being consistent (e.g. following the same rules as the parents for things like discipline, rewards, sweets).

7 Avoiding confrontations as far as possible.

8 Encouraging the child's cooperation by using songs, rhymes and games to make routines more fun.

9 Asking the child to help you (e.g. showing you where things are kept around the house or showing you the way to school).

10 Being tolerant and patient – do not force the child to participate in activities; they will join in when they are ready.

Sharing information with parents

Sharing information is an essential part of working with young children and their parents. Parents know more than you do about their children and their children's needs, so it is important that you listen to what the parents have to say. You must ensure that you have essential information from the parents, including:

❋ routine information – the child's medical history, including any medical conditions such as asthma, diabetes, epilepsy or allergies; the child's likes and dislikes; cultural or religious practices, which may have implications for the care of the child, such as special diets

❋ emergency information – contact numbers for the parents and the child's GP

❋ other relevant information – factors in the child's life that may affect their behaviour, including family difficulties and crises, such as divorce or bereavement.

Always remember confidentiality with regard to any information provided by the parents (see chapter 6).

Sort out how you will share information about the child with the parents (e.g. keeping a diary or daily log of the child's day, including food/drink intake, hours slept, play and early learning activities done, any developmental progress made). You could also make a brief note of any specific plans for the next day (e.g. going swimming or to the library). The parents can also use the diary/daily log to share information with you (e.g. if the child did not sleep well the night before, reminders about immunizations, dental check-ups or returning library books).

When the child passes back into the care of their parents each day, you should make time to chat briefly with the parents. They can read the detailed information about their child's day in the diary/daily log later on (see chapter 6).

Maintaining the child's usual routines

In the first week(s) it is essential to maintain the child's usual daily routine as far as possible, in order to provide the child with the consistency and security of having a recognized pattern to the day. Young children dislike changes or disruption to their routine. Routines are therefore especially important during transitional periods.

When you start work for a new family it will help if you can keep many of the child's daily routines the same. It is important that you try to keep to the child's regular routines, including feeding/mealtimes, nappy changing/toileting, bath-time, naps and/or bedtime.

You should get some idea of the child's usual daily routine on the first day (if not before) and stick to it. You should not try to establish any new routines during the settling-in period. The child has enough to cope with getting used to a new carer without changes to their routine as well.

Do not worry if the child is reluctant to spend time with you or participate in routines and activities. Remember it takes time for young children to adjust to having someone new looking after them.

The first week

Your first day will be spent familiarizing yourself with the house and the family's routines.

Usually one of the parents will stay at home with you during the first couple of days or first week. This helps to make the transition much easier, especially for the child, who has a familiar person around while getting used to you as the new nanny. During the first week the parent can provide you with essential information about:

* the layout of the house
* the household chores you are expected to carry out
* the child's usual routine, including mealtimes, sleeping patterns etc.
* the child's likes and dislikes regarding food, clothes, toys and activities.

If you are new to the area, the parents may help you to familiarize yourself with the local area by showing you the location of the child's nursery/school, local shops, park, library, leisure centre. Get an A–Z street plan to help you find your way around. You can also go to the local library or information centre to pick up leaflets about local attractions and activities suitable for young children.

Sometimes the nanny who is leaving will be asked to stay on during your first week. The previous nanny can help you with your workload while you are familiarizing yourself with your new working environment. One of the advantages of having the previous nanny around during the first week is that they usually have more time than the parents to show you the ropes.

However, there are some disadvantages to having the previous nanny around in the early days. For example, it can make the transition more difficult for the child, who may resent you and prefer to be with the previous nanny. Or you may feel intimidated by the other nanny's presence, especially if they appear super-efficient, and this in turn may knock your confidence.

Remember everyone feels awkward at first in a new job, but as you become familiar with the family and their routines you will soon develop confidence in your own skills and abilities.

Make sure you do the following during the first week:

* ensure the parents know the name and address of your next of kin (e.g. parent, spouse or partner) in case of emergencies
* make a list of contact numbers for emergencies (e.g. the parents' work and mobile telephone numbers, the child's GP, contact details of a close relative – grandparent, aunt or uncle – in case the child's parents cannot be contacted)
* ask about the location of the first aid box, fuse box and stopcock (to turn off water in case of burst pipe)
* make a note of the child's usual daily routine (e.g. mealtimes, naps)
* find out how to use the household appliances (e.g. cooker, washing machine, dishwasher)
* ask for a set of keys to the house
* make a note of any house rules (e.g. no smoking)
* find out your exact duties
* check which day is your payday and when your days off are.

Information about your exact duties, pay and days off will be stated in your contract. If you do not have a contract before you start work, make sure you get one from your employer as soon as possible (see chapter 4).

You should try to plan something pleasant to do on your first day off. Your first week is bound to be both tiring and challenging, so it helps to have something to look forward to, such as going out with friends or watching a favourite video.

Strategies for settling in

The first days (or even weeks) that young children spend in a new setting, situation or with a new carer require a sensitive approach from the adult(s) caring for them, as this enables them to cope with the separation from their parents and to adjust to any new routines and/or people.

You should remember the following key points:

＊ follow a clear, structured daily routine to provide stability and security for the child

＊ ensure the child's transition/comfort object is easily accessible

＊ provide play opportunities for the child to express feelings and concerns over separating from parents

＊ identify the child's individual needs

＊ provide activities and experiences appropriate to these needs

＊ show an active interest in the child's activities

＊ work with the child to establish clear boundaries and rules

＊ reassure the child about their parents' eventual return

＊ provide reminders of the child's parents (e.g. talk about them, point to photographs)

＊ encourage parental involvement as far as is practical and appropriate

＊ prepare parents for possible temporary effects of separation (e.g. the child may demonstrate feelings of anxiety by being clingy, hostile, aggressive or by regressing to a previous developmental level)

＊ encourage parents to be calm and relaxed to avoid the child sensing their anxiety (settling in can often be more stressful for the parents than the child).

EXERCISE: Plan possible activities to help a young child to settle in during your first week with a new family.

DAY	8.00 BREAKFAST	8.30 HELP CHILD DRESS	MORNING ACTIVITIES	10.00 SNACK	MORNING ACTIVITIES	NAP TIME (11.30)	12.30 LUNCH	AFTERNOON ACTIVITIES	2.30 SNACK	AFTERNOON ACTIVITIES	5.30 TEA	BABY-SITTING (6.00)
MONDAY	BREAKFAST	HELP CHILD DRESS	Ice breakers e.g. name games Mystery bag Construction toys	SNACK	Play in garden Story Rhymes/ songs	Child's washing Prepare lunch	LUNCH	Playgroup (meeting with parent exchange vital info).	SNACK	Playgroup Children's TV Prepare tea	TEA	
TUESDAY			Library (with parent)		Play in garden Story Rhymes/ songs	Child's ironing Prepare lunch		Painting Small-scale toys		Jigsaws Simple games Children's TV Prepare tea		
WEDNESDAY			Visit the park (with parent)		Construction toys Story Rhymes/ songs	Tidy child's bedroom Prepare lunch		Playgroup (local shopping with parent)		Playgroup Children's TV Prepare tea		
THURSDAY			Swimming (with parent)		Jigsaws Simple games Story Rhymes/ Songs	Wash swimming costumes etc. Prepare lunch		Play in garden Small-scale toys		Drawing/ colouring Make playdough Children's TV Prepare tea		Quiet games Bath time Bedtime Story
FRIDAY			Junk modelling Playdough		Play in garden Story Rhymes/ songs	Clean child's bedroom Prepare lunch		Playgroup (stay as adult helper)		Playgroup Children's TV Prepare tea		

Sample timetable of routines and play activities for the first week

MANAGING YOUR TIME

Managing your time effectively involves being clear about what you need to do and that you are able to do it. Unrealistic goals (especially in a new job) can lead to unnecessary stress, feeling overwhelmed, chores piling up, disagreements or arguments.

15 ways to manage your time more effectively

1 Decide to use time more effectively.
2 Check what you need to do, then prioritize: urgent/essential down to unimportant.
3 Make 'to do' lists in order of priority.
4 Estimate realistically the time needed for tasks.
5 Say 'no' if you cannot do a task in the time specified.
6 Forward plan using a good diary.
7 Organize how you intend to do each task.
8 Do the task!
9 Monitor or revise plans if necessary.
10 Be punctual and reliable.
11 Get a good watch with an alarm you can set to remind you of important times.
12 Remember 'A place for everything and everything in its place'!
13 Keep everything you need for specific tasks in one place (e.g. painting materials).
14 Store items you use regularly in accessible places.
15 Throw away rubbish.

EXERCISE: How do you manage your time to include your current work duties, any study requirements and home/family commitments? Think of ways you could manage your time more effectively.

THE PROBATIONARY PERIOD

As part of your contract you will have agreed a probationary period to allow you and the family to try out arrangements before you both commit yourselves to a more permanent agreement. If during the probationary period (usually about four weeks) you decide that you really do not wish to continue in this job, you can terminate the employment by giving one week's notice in writing. Think carefully about your reasons for leaving before you do this: is the problem a temporary one (e.g. difficult behaviour from the child during the transitional period) or is it something that cannot be resolved (e.g. your views on discipline are totally incompatible with those of the parents)?

Further reading

Bartholomew, L. and Bruce, T., 1993, *Getting To Know You: a guide to record keeping in early childhood education and care*, Hodder and Stoughton.

Gibson, R., 1998, *Usborne Playtime Activities*, Usborne Publishing Ltd.

Hobart, C. and Frankel, J., 1999, *A Practical Guide to Activities for Young Children*, 2nd edition, Nelson Thornes.

Matterson, E. (ed.), 1991, *This Little Puffin ... Finger Plays and Nursery Games*, Puffin Books.

Meggit, C., 1999, *Caring for Babies: a practical guide*, Hodder and Stoughton.

Mort, L. and Morris, J., 1989, *Bright Ideas for Early Years: getting started*, Scholastic.

Petrie, P., 1989, *Communicating with Children and Adults: interpersonal skills for those working with babies and children*, Hodder Arnold.

Professional relationships with employers 6

* Roles and boundaries
* Different parenting styles and skills
* Teamwork
* Effective communication
* Providing regular feedback
* Job performance reviews
* Nanny code of conduct
* Possible problems
* Resolving difficulties or conflicts
* Special situations

ROLES AND BOUNDARIES

As a nanny working in a family home you have a unique role compared with other childcare professionals. Working in a family home is different from other childcare settings because you are:

* caring for a child/children on a one-to-one basis
* working more closely with the parents
* being employed by the parents
* working independently without the support of colleagues.

To establish a professional relationship with the parents you need to understand clearly the roles and boundaries of everyone involved. Not only are the parents your employers, but you are also working together to provide the best care for their child or children.

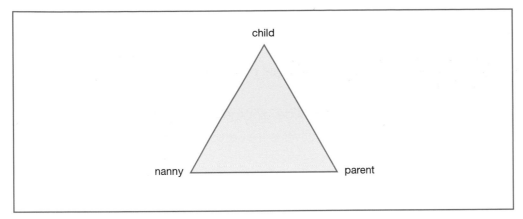

The nanny/child relationship

Your relationship with the child is the central part of your role as a nanny. This relationship involves:

❋ creating and maintaining a safe and healthy environment for the child

❋ being sensitive to the child's individual needs

❋ providing for the physical, emotional, intellectual, language and social needs of the child by using developmentally appropriate play/learning activities, materials and equipment (see below)

❋ providing praise and encouragement for the child's development and learning

❋ having a warm, friendly and caring attitude

❋ showing an active interest in the child's activities, including asking about their day at nursery/school, listening to them read and helping with homework

❋ performing domestic tasks related to the care and maintenance of the child's areas of the home, such as bedroom, playroom, bathroom and outside play space; laundering and making simple repairs to children's clothing; and observing safety rules in the home.

The most essential aspect of developing a positive relationship with the child involves your role and responsibilities for providing routines and activities that will help to meet *all* the child's developmental needs: social, physical, intellectual, communication and emotional.

Five ways to meet a child's developmental needs

Providing routines and activities to meet the child's developmental needs includes:

1   Encouraging and extending the child's social skills by:

❋ fostering self-reliance and independence through the practice of daily routines

❋ promoting positive behaviour through appropriate behaviour management techniques

* setting clear boundaries and rules in accordance with the parents' wishes
* encouraging socialization by providing opportunities to meet other babies and/or young children
* providing opportunities for social play.

(See chapter 9.)

2   Promoting the child's physical development by:

* providing routines and activities that are appropriate to age and level of development
* serving nutritious meals and snacks; remember to continue parents' feeding plan (e.g. bottle-feeding, weaning)
* seeing to the child's toileting needs (e.g. nappy changing, potty training)
* supervising rest periods, naps and sleep
* providing opportunities for fresh air and exercise, including outdoor play and outings
* protecting the child from infection and injury (e.g. ensuring immunizations are up-to-date, recognizing symptoms of common childhood illnesses, handling emergency situations and administering first aid)
* teaching child appropriate standards of cleanliness, including the hygienic way to bath and wash hands, brush hair and clean teeth
* taking every safety precaution when travelling with the child
* ensuring the child is dressed appropriately (e.g. wearing warm clothes in cold weather, wearing a hat in sunny weather and applying sunscreen).

(See chapters 7 and 8.)

3   Encouraging and extending the child's intellectual development by:

* providing play activities and learning experiences that are appropriate to the child's age and level of development
* providing toys and other play equipment that are age-appropriate to stimulate the child's thinking and learning
* providing opportunities to explore and learn about their environment (e.g. outings such as shopping trips, library visits, going to the park)
* sharing books, stories, rhymes and songs to stimulate new ideas and consolidate existing learning.

(See chapters 8 and 10.)

4   Encouraging and extending the child's language/communication skills by:

* communicating effectively at the child's level of understanding
* modelling appropriate language for the child
* recognizing stages of language development in young children
* engaging in activities that encourage the child's language development
* listening carefully to the child's talk and responding appropriately
* considering the mood of the child (e.g. sometimes will not want to talk)

* providing opportunities for language, including participating in everyday conversations, sharing books and stories, singing rhymes and songs.

(See chapter 8.)

5 Promoting the child's emotional wellbeing by:

* helping the child to cope with the transitions of the parent(s) going to work and of being cared for by a new nanny
* helping the child to cope with other transitions as they occur (e.g. starting nursery/school, moving house, arrival of new baby)
* respecting each child as a unique individual
* creating an environment that fosters the child's trust and self-esteem
* providing continuity and consistency of care by continuing the child's usual routine (as far as possible and in conjunction with the parents' wishes) to give the child emotional security and reassurance
* providing stimulating play activities to promote emotional well-being
* using praise and encouragement for the child's efforts and achievements to develop the child's self-confidence and promote positive self-esteem.

(See chapter 9.)

The nanny/parent relationship

Everyone benefits when the nanny and the parents develop an effective and positive working relationship. The child thrives when there is continuity of care from the adults who are most important in their lives. The parents' trust in you grows when the parent/nanny partnership is working well. A harmonious working relationship enables you to promote the child's physical and emotional well being to the fullest extent and gives you better job satisfaction.

A good working relationship between you and the parents begins with fair terms of employment, benefits and incentives, and a contract that defines both your expectations and those of the parents as regards your duties, wages, hours and working conditions (see chapter 4).

To develop positive relationships with the parents you need to:

* work cooperatively with them
* perform your duties as agreed
* communicate openly and effectively
* show sensitivity to family situations
* seek constructive solutions to problems
* maintain a consistent, positive attitude.

You should be a sympathetic listener if the parents wish to talk over their feelings of concern, anxiety or even guilt about leaving their child in someone else's care. You can also talk to them about current childcare theories and development issues to reassure the parents that their child is getting the very best in substitute care.

Five ways to develop positive relationships with the parents

The following guidelines may help you to foster positive relationships with the parents:

1 Exchange information with the parents:
   * communication is the key to fostering a good relationship with the parents
   * take a few minutes each day to talk with the parents and keep a daily log
   * keep the lines of communication open and deal with any problems as they occur, before they get out of hand.

2 Understand your role as a nanny:
   * the roles of the nanny and the parent must not be confused
   * you are there to complement the parents, not to replace them
   * while you may be in charge of the child's daily routines and activities, the parents will usually decide if the child can invite a friend for tea or spend some pocket money.

3 Respect the family's right to privacy:
   * all matters relating to the family should be treated as private and confidential
   * your employer needs to feel that you are trustworthy and will not gossip about them
   * in the very rare circumstance that you are concerned about a child's welfare, you should follow the usual child protection procedures (see chapter 7).

4 Support your employer's parenting style:
   * recognize the ultimate authority of parents in making decisions about the welfare and care of their child/children
   * respect the parents' philosophy of childrearing
   * acknowledge the values, needs and ideas of the parents when there is disagreement about childrearing issues
   * your professional expertise must not be used to impose your ideas on the parents; instead try to work *with* the parents to reach a reasonable compromise.

5 Develop a partnership with parents:
   * a partnership between you and the parents helps strengthen the nanny/parent relationship and provides the child with consistency
   * young children become confused when they receive contradictory messages from you and a parent
   * you and the parents should discuss and agree on how you will all respond to certain situations before the situations arise
   * consistency over behaviour and discipline is particularly important (see chapter 9).

The parent/child relationship

Suspicions that the child will become closer to the nanny than to the parent (unfounded or not) can undermine the relationship between you and the parents, especially the mother. You must never compete or seem to be competing with the parents for the child's affections. You must always support the parent/child relationship.

You should help with essential household chores, such as the child's laundry, child's meals, maintenance of the child's clothes and equipment and cleaning the child's bedroom. This will allow the parents to spend more quality time with their child when they are not at work.

Five ways to provide support for the parent/child relationship

You can help to support a positive parent/child relationship in the following ways:

1　Help to create daily rituals that both child and parent can enjoy:
   ❋ making and eating breakfast together in the morning
   ❋ sharing a short mid-afternoon phone conversation
   ❋ reading a bedtime story
   ❋ do not do that particular task unless the parent specifically asks you to do it instead of them.

2　Involve the parents in planning the child's day:
   ❋ listen to their suggestions for outings and projects or after-school activities
   ❋ discuss the day's plans with the parents each morning
   ❋ debrief the parents at the end of the day
   ❋ keep a daily log of the day's activities and events
   ❋ have regular meetings to discuss the decisions and choices either of you wish to make regarding the child's activities (see below).

3　Be sensitive during the handover period at the end of the day:
   ❋ give the child time to adjust when the parents return home in the evening
   ❋ let them join the activity you and the child are engaged in
   ❋ do not go off with the parent to debrief and leave the child alone during this difficult transition time
   ❋ arrange the schedule so you do not have to rush off as soon as the parent gets home from work – try to have a 15-minute overlap.

4　Do not try to take over the parents' roles:
   ❋ do not try to be the parent – remember your role as a nanny is to complement and support the parent's role
   ❋ develop outside relationships to broaden your perspective
   ❋ meet other nannies and join a nanny support group, as this will help you to gain a better understanding of your role as a nanny (see chapter 11).

5 Do not try to undermine the parents' authority
   ❊ follow the parents' wishes regarding the child's behaviour and discipline
   ❊ follow any house rules (e.g. tidying up after activities)
   ❊ follow the parents' rules regarding eating sweets, watching TV programmes, playing computer games etc.

Your professional commitment to children

As a professional nanny you should act as an advocate for young children. You should actively promote knowledge and understanding of young children, including their needs and rights. You should be familiar with the signs of child abuse and neglect and be knowledgeable about the procedures for dealing with them (see chapter 7).

You should become involved in social, cultural and educational activities, not only to maintain and improve your childcare skills, but also to enhance your own personal growth. Try to participate in personal and professional growth activities, such as:

❊ studying for (additional) childcare and education qualifications
❊ attending seminars and workshops on the care and education of young children
❊ participating in nanny-related organizations (e.g. nanny networks, PANN)
❊ being involved in community affairs and child advocacy groups.

DIFFERENT PARENTING STYLES AND SKILLS

While all parents are individuals and have a unique relationship with their children, three general styles of parenting have been identified:

❊ authoritative
❊ authoritarian
❊ permissive.

One of these three main parenting styles usually emerges during the child's pre-school years. No parent has an absolutely consistent parenting style across all situations. However, parents usually demonstrate the same tendencies in their approach to childrearing. These three parenting styles are also linked to different behaviours and personality traits of children.

1 Authoritative parenting style
   ❊ Parent's behaviour
      a. allows their child quite a bit of freedom
      b. has clear standards of behaviour
      c. reasons with their child and listens to their views

d. is not afraid to insist on specific behaviours

e. sets firm limits and sticks to them

f. is sensitive to their child's needs and views

g. is quick to praise their child's efforts and achievements

h. has clear expectations for their child

i. disciplines with love and affection, rather than power

j. explains rules and expectations to their child rather than just asserting them.

❋ Child's behaviour

a. is happy, self-reliant and able to cope with stress

b. has warm relationships with parents

c. tends to be popular with peers

d. has confidence and good social skills

e. tends to set own standards for behaviour

f. is goal- and achievement-orientated.

2 Authoritarian parenting style

❋ Parent's behaviour

a. expects child to behave at all times

b. enforces rules rigidly but often does not explain these clearly

c. ignores child's wishes or opinions

d. expects unquestioning obedience and respect for authority

e. delivers harsh consequences for child's misbehaviour

f. relies on physical punishment and withdrawal of affection.

❋ Child's behaviour

a. tends to be obedient and orderly

b. has low self-esteem and poor self-control

c. has distant relationship with parents

d. may be aggressive and lose interest in school earlier (especially boys)

e. tends to be motivated by reward or fear of punishment rather than because it's the right thing to do.

3 Permissive parenting style

❋ Parent's behaviour

a. allows their child to have free expression

b. does not enforce clear rules on acceptable/unacceptable behaviour

c. accepts or ignores bad behaviour

d. makes few demands on their child for mature independent behaviour

e. sets limits by reasoning with their child rather than asserting wishes

f. has few expectations of their child

g. imposes little discipline.

* Child's behaviour
    a. can appear happy
    b. has warm relationship with parents
    c. does not cope with stress very well
    d. gets angry if they do not get their own way
    e. tends to be immature
    f. can be aggressive and domineering with their peers
    g. tends not to be goal- and achievement-orientated.

Most parents show traits of all three parenting styles. How parents interact with their child will depend on a number of things, including:

* the particular situation
* the parent's mood
* the child's mood
* the parent's temperament
* the child's temperament
* the parent's own experiences in childhood
* other factors, such as work pressures or family crises.

TEAMWORK

Much of adult life involves working with other people, usually in a group or team. Individuals within a team affect each other in various ways. Within the team there will be complex interactions involving different personalities, roles and expectations, as well as hidden agendas that influence the behaviour of individual members of the team. Teamwork is essential when working closely and regularly with other people over a long period of time, such as working with parents as a nanny in a family home.

Teamwork is important because it helps you to:

* **t**ake effective action when planning agreed routines and activities
* **e**fficiently implement the agreed routines and activities
* **a**gree aims and values regarding the child's care and education
* **m**otivate and support each other
* **w**elcome feedback about your work
* **o**ffer additional support in times of stress
* **r**eflect on and evaluate your own working practices
* **k**now and use your personal strengths and skills.

EFFECTIVE COMMUNICATION

Effective communication is essential for developing effective teamwork. Effective lines of communication are also important to ensure that you and the parents receive the necessary up-to-date information to enable you both to make a full contribution to the care and education of the child.

The first step towards effective communication with other people is being able to listen attentively to what they have to say. Nearly all breakdowns in communication are due to people not listening to each other. Effective communication requires good interpersonal skills, such as:

* being available – make time to talk with the parents
* being an attentive listener – concentrate on what the parents are saying
* using appropriate non-verbal skills (e.g. face the parents, lean slightly towards them, smile, nod, use open-handed gestures, not clenched fists)
* following the rules of turn-taking in language exchanges – every person needs to have their say while others listen
* being polite and courteous – no shouting, no talking over other people, avoiding sarcasm
* being relaxed, confident and articulate
* using appropriate vocabulary for your listener(s)
* encouraging others to talk by asking 'open' questions
* responding positively to what is said
* being receptive to new ideas
* being sympathetic to other viewpoints (even if you totally disagree with them!)
* providing opportunities for meaningful communication to take place (e.g. regular meetings).

PROVIDING REGULAR FEEDBACK

Effective communication is the key to a rewarding and positive relationship with the child and their parents. Regular feedback through daily reports, the daily log/diary and scheduled meetings will lead to better organization of routines and activities, which will mean less stress for everyone and a smoother-running household.

Daily reports

You should take the time each day to talk briefly with the parents when you hand the child back into their care. You should keep the conversation short so that the child can interact with the parents as soon as possible. You can put more detailed information about the child's day in the daily log, which can be read later by the parents (see below). In your daily report you should tell the parents about significant events of the day (e.g. if the child was ill, upset or had a minor accident/injury), changes in the child's usual behaviour or any developmental progress. By keeping the lines of communication open and dealing with any problems as they occur, before they get out of hand, you will maintain a positive relationship with the parents.

Keeping a daily log or diary of the child's day is the best way to share detailed information about the child with the parents; this might include:

✳ notes and reminders from the parents

✳ the child's food and drink intake

✳ nap times and hours slept

✳ play and early learning activities done

✳ any developmental progress made

✳ any medication and when administered

✳ any mishaps (e.g. minor injuries, toileting 'accidents')

✳ notes to parents about plans for the next day (e.g. going swimming).

Here is a sample layout for a daily log:

Daily log

Date: ....

Nanny start time: .... Nanny finish time: ....

1 Parent notes and reminders to nanny: ....

2 Meals (including the child's food and drink intake):

✳ Breakfast: ....

✳ Mid-morning snack: ....

✳ Lunch: ....

✳ Mid-afternoon snack: ....

✳ Dinner: ....

3 Nap times (including hours slept): ....

4 Nappy/toileting: ....

5 Play and early learning activities: ....

....

6 Developmental progress: ....

7 Medication: ....

8 Mishaps: ....

9 Kitty/expenses/mileage: ....

10 Nanny notes to parents: ....

....

Regular parent/nanny meetings

As a nanny you should have regular meetings with the parents. Perhaps have weekly meetings during your probationary period (e.g. the first month) and then monthly after that. If anything needs to be discussed in between the scheduled meetings, you can mention this when giving your daily report.

These meetings will enable you to make relevant contributions to provide more effective support for both the child and the parents. You may discuss specific routines and activities the parents wish you to carry out, as well as plans you have to encourage and/or extend their child's development and learning. Try to have these meetings when the child is otherwise engaged (e.g. playing with friends, in bed asleep). It is essential that both you and the parents are able to speak your minds without the possibility of the child overhearing what is said and becoming worried as a result.

You need to prepare for such meetings carefully; make sure you have all the relevant information (e.g. the daily log/diary, activity file and any notes on the child's developmental progress). At the meeting express your opinions in a clear, concise manner and demonstrate respect for the contributions made by the parents. Make notes during the meeting to remind yourself of any action *you* need to take as a result of the issues discussed.

JOB PERFORMANCE REVIEWS

You can use your contract and/or job description as the basis for a job performance review. A review of your contract/job description will help to clarify your exact duties and responsibilities, especially if any disagreements occur between you and the parents. It is a good idea to have a review at the end of your probationary period (e.g. after the first month) and again after six months, along with a salary review. Suggest a review to the parents if they have not thought of it already. A pre-planned review, before any particular issues arise, can make the meeting more relaxed and place you and the parents in less defensive positions.

NANNY CODE OF CONDUCT

As a nanny you should consider yourself to be a professional childcarer. Being a professional childcarer means that you should behave in a reliable and honest manner that will inspire the parents with respect, trust and confidence in your abilities. You should always endeavour to:

✳ promote the child's social, physical, intellectual, communication and emotional development
✳ respect and support the parents in the task of nurturing and caring for their child
✳ maintain high standards of professional conduct
✳ seek personal growth and professional development.

Professional practice

The Professional Association of Nursery Nurses (PANN) has a Code of Practice for its members. The code provides guidance for all practising professional childcarers in carrying out their duties and responsibilities. You will find it useful to bear in mind these guidelines when working with young children and their families.

The PANN Code of Practice

THE BASIC PRINCIPLE IS THAT THE INTEREST OF THE CHILD IS PLACED BEFORE ALL ELSE.

Members should:

* value and respect each child as an individual
* be aware of, and safeguard, the rights of all children
* facilitate and promote the growth and development of the whole child
* be aware of, and endeavour to meet, the needs of each child for whom they are professionally responsible.

The child within the family

Members should:

* see the child in the context of his or her family situation and be aware of differences in family structures in our society
* be aware that the care of the child is a shared responsibility, which must take account of the customs, values and beliefs of the family or the main carers
* work in a cooperative and collaborative manner with the family to promote and safeguard the wellbeing of the child/children.

Professional practice

Members should:

* ensure that no action is taken, or omission made, which is detrimental to the welfare and safety of, or that hinders the development of, the child, for example, strike action
* maintain the highest possible standards of performance, and aim to improve their knowledge, skills and competencies by taking advantage of in-service and other training
* constantly evaluate and reappraise their own methods, policies and practices and be aware of the need to keep up-to-date with current developments in the light of changing needs and circumstances
* be aware of the need for confidentiality within their professional practice. Confidential information received should not be disclosed unless required by law or to protect the interests or welfare of the child.

Working with others

Members should:

* work in a cooperative manner with other professionals in the care and education of all children

* acknowledge and respect the contribution of other colleagues who share in the provision of the service

* share their knowledge, demonstrate their skills with students and other colleagues to develop and promote good childcare practice whilst offering guidance and support as appropriate

* be prepared to give support and supervision to, and receive support and supervision from, colleagues and management to further their own personal and professional development and that of the service.

MEMBERS SHOULD AT ALL TIMES ACTIVELY PROMOTE, AND TAKE ALL OPPORTUNITIES TO IMPROVE, THE STATUS OF THE PROFESSION.

(PANN 2004)

Reviewing your professional practice

You need to know and understand clearly the exact role and responsibilities of your work as a nanny. Review your professional practice by making regular and realistic assessments of how well your working practices match your role and responsibilities.

Self-evaluation is needed to improve your own professional practice and to develop your ability to reflect upon activities and modify plans to meet the needs of the child. When evaluating your own practice you should consider the following points:

* Was your own contribution appropriate? Did you choose the right time, place and resources? Did you intervene enough or too much?

* Did you achieve your goals (e.g. objectives for the child and yourself)? If not, why not? Were the goals too ambitious or unrealistic?

* What other strategies/methods could have been used? Suggest possible modifications.

* Whom should you ask for further advice (e.g. the parents, other nannies)?

Share your self-assessments with the parents during your regular meetings and/or job performance reviews. You should also ask the parents for feedback about how well you fulfil the requirements and expectations of your role. You can also reflect on your own professional practice by making comparisons with appropriate models of good practice (e.g. the work of more experienced nannies).

Developing effective practice

To develop your effectiveness in your role as a nanny, you should be able to identify your own personal development objectives:

* **s**pecific
* **m**easurable
* **a**chievable
* **r**ealistic
* **t**ime-bound.

You should discuss and agree these objectives with the parents. You may consider that some of your duties require modification or improvement and discuss possible changes with the parents. Or you may feel that you lack sufficient knowledge and skills to implement particular activities and need to discuss opportunities for you to undertake the relevant training (e.g. updating first aid skills). To achieve your personal development objectives you should make effective use of the people, resources and other development or training opportunities available to you.

Your professional portfolio, which highlights your existing experience and qualifications, can form the basis for assessing your training needs. This portfolio will also be a tangible record of your professional development and will help to boost your self-esteem.

Training opportunities

When assessing your personal development and training needs you need to consider:

* your existing experience and skills
* the needs of the child and their parents
* any problems with how you currently work
* any new or changing expectations for your role (e.g. the child starting nursery/school or the arrival of a new baby).

You may wish to update your knowledge and skills through short courses, such as paediatric first aid, food handling and hygiene, health and safety, child protection awareness, managing children's behaviour or children with special needs (see chapter 2).

EXERCISE: Review and assess your own work performance. Find out about the professional development and training opportunities available for nannies in your local area.

Confidentiality

You may find that the parents will want to talk to you about their problems or give you details about their family. If it is something that will affect the child (e.g. the parents are going through a divorce), the parents should have an honest conversation with you about it so that you can provide additional support for the child during a difficult transitional period. Private family matters that do not directly affect the child are not your concern.

Any information given to you by the parents should be considered private and confidential – you must not gossip about it. However, if you think the child is at risk, you must pass on confidential information to an appropriate person (e.g. your local social services department, the NSPCC or the police) and tell them about your concerns.

Remember, if you are in any doubt, it is much better to talk to a person with experience of working with children who will be able to advise you (e.g. talk to your GP first without revealing the identity of the child). Remember that the family has a right to privacy and you should only pass on information in the genuine interests of the child or to safeguard their welfare. (See chapter 7 for more information about child protection issues.)

Confidentiality is also important with regard to the daily log and anything discussed or noted down at your meetings with the parents. Except where a child is potentially at risk, information should not be given to other agencies unless previously agreed.

The parents should also respect your right to privacy (especially if you are a live-in nanny) and should not discuss your habits or flaws with anyone else. Aspects of your life that do not affect the care of the child or the conditions under which you were employed should be of no concern to your employer. The parents should give you the same privacy to pursue your own personal life as they would expect to receive in similar circumstances.

Professional detachment

When working as a nanny it is impossible to be emotionally detached – if you were, you would not be a good nanny. To work well as a nanny involves genuinely caring about the child. In addition to meeting the child's physical and intellectual needs, you also need to provide emotional security by showing a genuine interest in everything the child says and does, as well as providing comfort when the child is upset or unwell. Children can sense when they are with someone who really cares about them. However, always remember that the child is not yours and never let the child call you mummy or daddy. Very young children may do this, especially if you have cared for them since babyhood. Give the child a gentle reminder of your proper name, point to a photograph of their parents and say, 'This is mummy and this is daddy.'

You must also make a clear distinction between your relationship with the family and your relationship with your own family. This can be quite difficult at times, especially if you are a live-in nanny. You should be able to share in the different aspects of the family's life (such as mealtimes, birthdays and other special occasions) without compromising your professionalism. Though you may share the highs and lows of the family's life, you must maintain some detachment to be an effective nanny. Personal friendships with the parents, other family members or friends of the family are best avoided as they can complicate the nanny/parent relationship and confuse the child.

Professional appearance and manner

Working as a nanny in a private family home is obviously less formal than working in other childcare settings (e.g. in a day nursery you might have to wear a uniform). However, it is still important to have a professional appearance and manner – after all, you are a childcare professional.

The professional nanny

12 ways to demonstrate that you are a professional nanny

You should remember these important points:

1 Be punctual – if you are late, you will make the parents late for work and/or cause rushing about, which creates an unsettling start to the day for everyone.

2 Dress professionally, comfortably and safely (e.g. no high heels or dangling earrings).

3 Tie back long hair and keep fingernails short (especially if working with babies).

4 Be flexible – all families have differing lifestyles and childrearing practices.

5 Look alert and interested in the child's routines and activities.

6 Ensure you are physically at the same level as the child during activities.

7 Use friendly but professional speech (e.g. never use slang or swear words).

8 Tidy up equipment and materials after use.

9 Be aware of safety at all times (see chapter 7).

10 Remember to record events in the daily log.

11 Do not smoke at work (try to give up completely if you can).

12 Do not rush off at the end of the day – always give the parents a brief report about the child and the day's events before you go home or return to your own room.

POSSIBLE PROBLEMS

Everyone experiences problems during their working lives. Most problems occur at the beginning of a working relationship when each person is trying to establish their new roles and responsibilities. Here are some of the possible problems you may encounter in your work as a nanny:

* parents who take you for granted by coming home late a lot and expecting more hours than stated in your contract (without paid overtime or advance notice)

* parents who always expect you to be available on weekends and evenings (especially a live-in nanny) when this was not agreed in your contract

* parents who give you extra duties and responsibilities (e.g. domestic chores for the whole family, not just those connected with the care of the child/children) without negotiating additional perks or increased wages

* parents who do not provide you with positive feedback about your work

* parents who offer your professional services to a friend or neighbour without checking with you first

* parents who resent their child's attachment to you

* children who demonstrate difficult or challenging behaviour (e.g. disregarding your authority or displaying antisocial behaviour)

* parents who do not show respect for your authority by not speaking to or disciplining their children when they ignore your instructions or are disrespectful to you

* parents who have conflicting views over childrearing practices (e.g. discipline – remember your professional commitment to the no smacking rule)

* parents who express attitudes that conflict with your own values (e.g. making overly political, racist or sexist remarks).

RESOLVING DIFFICULTIES OR CONFLICTS

As a nanny, you need to be able to recognize and respond to any problems that affect your ability to work effectively. This includes dealing appropriately with difficulties and conflictive situations that affect your working relationships with the family.

Conflicts and difficulties are a part of everyone's working lives. Most conflicts are usually minor and quickly resolved, especially when people work together effectively as a team (see section on teamwork above). If communication and working relationships break down, conflict situations can arise which seriously damage the atmosphere in the family home. Conflicts can occur between: you and the child/children; you and the parents; the child/children and their parents.

Most conflicts involving work as a nanny arise due to:

❋ concerns about duties and responsibilities

❋ disputes over pay and conditions

❋ disagreements about childrearing practices (especially discipline)

❋ clashes concerning different lifestyle choices (especially for live-in nannies).

Conflicts can also arise due to prejudice or discrimination; evidence of such attitudes or behaviour must be challenged, as they are not only undesirable but also unlawful.

Many difficulties and conflicts can be resolved through open and honest discussion. This will involve arranging a mutually convenient time to talk to the parents about the problem.

Remember these important points:

1 focus on the facts by stating the exact nature of the problem

2 avoid making personal comments (be tactful!)

3 suggest a possible and practical solution

4 be prepared to compromise if at all possible.

The best way to resolve conflicts is to be assertive by discussing and negotiating a compromise that suits everyone to bring about a win-win solution to the problem. Remember, compromise equals wise!

EXERCISE: Think about how you have responded (or could respond) to a conflictive situation. Check your contract to see if there is a section about grievances.

Where serious difficulties or conflict situations cannot be resolved, your contract should state how any grievances would be dealt with. If the matter cannot be resolved or a compromise agreed upon, you may need to consider resigning from the job (see chapter 12).

SPECIAL SITUATIONS

There are a number of special situations that may affect your professional relationship with the child and/or their parents. These include:

* parental separation or divorce
* terminal illness or death in the family
* child abuse and neglect (see chapter 7)
* domestic violence
* sexual harassment
* moving house (see chapter 11).

Parental separation or divorce

If the child's parents are experiencing a marital breakdown, your role will be to support the child through the very difficult transition if their parents separate or divorce. You must not take the side of either parent or criticize them in front of the child. You may be asked to take on extra duties and responsibilities (for which you can expect to be paid more money).

For babies facing their parents' separation or divorce, the loss of constant contact with one parent (usually the father) decreases the amount of stimulation from the outside world. From the age of one year onwards, parental separation or divorce affects the child much more directly because the child loses regular contact with someone they love and trust.

Young children aged between three and six years tend to blame themselves for their parents' separation or divorce. The child will often try to find easy solutions to mend their parents' divorce (e.g. behaving especially well or drawing nice pictures to bring daddy home).

Older children (from six years old) tend to cope with their parents' separation and divorce far better than very young children because they have stronger peer relations and usually have some understanding of the reasons for the divorce, so do not tend to blame themselves (Hines 2002).

During separation or divorce the child's parents may be facing overwhelming stress and their parenting skills may diminish because of their own difficulties in dealing with the transition. Both parents may become distant, less affectionate and may lack consistent control over their child. You should try to give the child additional attention and comfort, especially if the child is going through another transition at the same time, such as starting nursery or school.

Terminal illness or death in the family

A terminal illness or death in the family is difficult to cope with for everyone concerned. You may need to provide additional care and support for the child (and the parent) if one of the parents or other close family member has a terminal illness or dies. You should remember to treat the child with extra care and sensitivity during this difficult time.

How children cope with change or loss depends on their personalities and the way their parents or carers support them through the transition. Young children grieve on the death of a loved one and experience the same feelings as bereaved adults. However, because young children's levels of understanding about death vary, it may be difficult to understand their feelings, especially in children aged five years and under. You need to understand that babies and toddlers do not truly understand about death, but react to the grief of other people around them (e.g. a grieving parent may convey sad feelings to the baby, who then responds by crying constantly). Older children may experience feelings such as shock, confusion, anger or guilt. They may not show their feelings openly, but changes in their usual behaviour patterns may indicate that they are suffering and require additional support. Common behaviour changes in a bereaved child include: becoming withdrawn or clingy, being aggressive, toileting 'accidents' or wetting the bed, poor concentration, bullying or being bullied.

The terminal illness or death of the child (especially a cot death) will be extremely difficult for everyone to cope with. You will need to come to terms with your own feelings of shock, sadness, anger and even misplaced guilt. There are many organizations that can help you and the family to cope at this difficult time (see Further reading).

Domestic violence

If you work with a family where there is evidence of domestic violence, your support for the victim of violence (usually the mother) could be vital. Always remember the safety of the child is paramount; if you have any concerns that the child is also experiencing violence, you should follow the usual child protection procedures (see chapter 7). Here are some useful points to remember when providing support to a parent in this situation:

✳ Approach her in an understanding, non-blaming way. Explain to her that she is not alone and that there are many women like her in the same situation. Acknowledge that it takes strength to trust someone enough to talk to them about experiencing abuse. Give her time to talk; don't push her to go into too much detail if she doesn't want to.

✳ Acknowledge that she is in a scary, difficult situation. Tell her that no one deserves to be threatened or beaten, despite what her abuser has told her. Nothing she can do or say can justify the abuser's behaviour.

✳ Support her as a friend. Be a good listener. Encourage her to express her hurt and anger. Allow her to make her own decisions, even if it means she isn't ready to leave the relationship. This is her decision.

* Ask if she has suffered physical harm. Offer to go with her to the hospital if she needs to go. Help her to report the assault to the police if she chooses to do so.
* Be ready to provide information on the help available to abused women and their children. Explore the available options with her. Go with her to visit a solicitor if she is ready to take this step.
* Plan safe strategies for leaving an abusive relationship. Let her create the boundaries of what is safe and what is not safe; don't encourage her to follow any strategies that she is expressing doubt about.
* Offer the use of your address and/or telephone number for information and messages relating to her situation.
* Look after yourself while you are supporting someone through such a difficult and emotional time. Ensure that you do not put yourself into a dangerous situation; for example, do not offer to talk to the abuser about her or let yourself be seen by the abuser as a threat to their relationship.

(Women's Aid 2003)

Sexual harassment

Sexual harassment is another difficult situation that you may have to deal with as a nanny.

What counts as sexual harassment?

* sexual demands by a person of your own or the opposite sex
* any behaviour of a sexual nature, which creates an intimidating, hostile or humiliating working environment for you
* indecent or dirty remarks
* comments about the way you look which you find demeaning
* questions about your sex life.

How to handle it:

* make it clear that you reject this treatment and record what has happened
* keep a diary of behaviour you find offensive, including times, dates, locations and any witnesses
* tell someone you trust
* tell your doctor if your health is suffering
* report the harassment to your employer (e.g. the other parent)
* contact your trade union (if you have one)
* if an employment service organized your placement, tell them
* in some cases you should contact the police – some forms of sexual harassment are a criminal offence.

Who can give you more advice?

❋ the Equal Opportunities Commission offers excellent advice online and in leaflet form, as well as having advisors

❋ the Citizens Advice Bureau.

Further reading

Abbott, L. and Moylett, H. (eds.), 1997, *Working with the Under Threes: training and professional development*, Open University Press.

Bartholomew, L. and Bruce, T., 1993, *Getting To Know You: a guide to record keeping in early childhood education and care*, Hodder and Stoughton.

Childline booklet, '*I can't stop feeling sad*', at www.childline.org.uk/BereavementReport.asp

Department of Health, Home Office and Department for Education and Employment, 1999, *Working Together to Safeguard Children*, HMSO.

Hobart, C. and Frankel, J., 2001, *Nannying: a guide to good practice*, Nelson Thornes.

Lindon, J., 2003, *Child Protection*, 2nd edition, Hodder and Stoughton.

Meggit, C. and Sunderland, G., 2000, *Child Development: an illustrated guide*, Heinemann Educational.

O'Hagan, M. and Smith, M., 1999, *Early Years Child Care and Education: key issues*, Bailliere Tindall.

Petrie, P., 1989, *Communicating with Children and Adults: interpersonal skills for those working with babies and children*, Hodder Arnold.

Professional Association of Nursery Nurses (PANN), 2002, *All You Need To Know About Working as a Nanny* (the booklet is available for a small charge).

Woolfson, R., 1999, *From Birth to Starting School: child development for nursery nurses*, *Nursery World* edition, Caring Books.

Child safety and security   7

❀ Establishing routines

❀ Maintaining children's safety

❀ First aid

❀ Common childhood illnesses and
health problems

❀ Child protection

ESTABLISHING ROUTINES

Routines are essential parts of the day for babies and young children. It is important that routines (e.g. mealtimes, nap-times, nappy changing, toileting, bath-time and bedtime) provide valuable opportunities for babies and young children to develop and learn as well as to interact positively with others.

Establishing routines involves providing physical care to help maintain young children's safety and security. You should establish carefully structured routines based on a sound knowledge of the child as an individual as well as the wishes of the child's parents. When establishing routines you should consider the child's age and level of development as well as the child's individual needs, interests and preferences.

When establishing and maintaining routines, remember these important points:

❀ talk, sing, smile and make eye contact with the child during routines

❀ know the child's personal preferences (e.g. how a baby likes to be held when being given a bottle, a child's favourite cup and cutlery, a child's favourite clothes)

❀ allow the child to be independent and practise new skills as appropriate to age and level of development

❀ involve the child in everyday tasks (e.g. loading the washing machine, making a snack or setting and clearing the table)

❀ use finger rhymes, songs and simple games to make routines more interesting and fun (e.g. singing 'This little piggy went to market…' works wonders when cutting the nails of a baby or toddler).

Maintaining routines

Once routines have been established they need to be maintained in order to provide young children with the consistency and security of having a recognized pattern to their day. Young children dislike changes or disruption to their routine. Routines are especially important during periods of change such as:

* getting a new nanny
* mother returning to work after maternity leave
* starting nursery or school
* arrival of new brother or sister
* visits to doctor, dentist or hospital
* family separation, bereavement or serious illness.

(There is more about helping children to cope with change and transitions in chapter 5.)

When you start working for a new family it will help if you can keep many of the child's daily routines the same. Mealtimes and nap-times are very important times of the day for young children and it is essential that you try to keep to the child's regular routine.

You will need to adapt a child's routines or establish new ones as the child grows and develops. For example, a nappy-changing routine will eventually become a toileting routine. Daily routines will also change when the child starts playgroup, nursery or school. Once the child starts school, after-school activities and clubs may mean more changes to the child's routine. Be consistent in your introduction of any new routines, as this will help the child to adjust to any changes more easily.

Mealtimes

You will need to follow any parental instructions regarding a baby's feeding times or a young child's mealtime routine. If the child already has an established routine then you should follow that. Sometimes the parents of a baby or very young child may want you to help establish a regular bottle-feeding or mealtime routine. You should remember that not everyone has the same diet. You must talk to the family about which foods are appropriate and which are not.

Most young children prefer plain and familiar food they can eat with their fingers, but they also need opportunities to develop the skills of using a spoon, fork and then knife. You should encourage children to use safe, child-sized versions of these, as appropriate to their age, level of development and culture.

A typical schedule for a young child's meals might be:

* breakfast
* mid-morning snack
* lunch
* mid-afternoon snack
* evening meal.

Baby being spoon-fed

Eight ways to encourage positive mealtime routines

1   Let children eat at their own pace. Allow extra time for younger children to eat, especially if they are still developing self-feeding skills.

2   Use child-sized equipment to facilitate eating and encourage self-feeding skills, e.g. highchair (with harness), booster seat, bibs, small cutlery.

3   Avoid linking food with behaviour, either as a reward or a punishment.

4   Mealtimes can be opportunities for children to be independent by choosing foods.

5   Encourage children to taste everything, but be careful not to force them to eat.

6   Remember some children eat more than others and the same child may eat differing amounts at different times, e.g. may eat less if tired, ill or upset; may eat more after energetic play or during a growth spurt.

7   Avoid allowing toys or television to distract the child during mealtimes.

8   Eat with the children and use the time to share the events of the day so far. Mealtimes should be pleasant and social occasions. Eating with an adult provides young children with a positive role model, e.g. seeing you enjoying food and trying new foods, observing table manners.

Rest and sleep

Remember that most babies and young children need lots of sleep. Here are some general guidelines about the approximate number of hours' sleep (including naps) the average young child needs at different ages. Every child is different, so some children will need more or less sleep than others.

Age	Night-time sleep (hours)	Daytime sleep (hours)	Total sleep (hours)
0–1 month	9	9 (4*)	18
1–6 months	8	7 (3*)	15
6–12 months	11	3 (2*)	14
1–2 years	11	2 (2*)	13
2–3 years	11	2 (1*)	13
3–4 years	11	1 (1*)	12
4–6 years	11	0	11
6–8 years	10	0	10

Number of naps

Nap-times

Nap-time can present some challenging moments. The routine can either convey warmth and security or stress and turmoil to young children. You cannot *make* a child sleep during the day, but you can create a relaxed and quiet time to rest. Some children may have trouble settling down at nap-time for a variety of reasons, including a transition or crisis in their lives, excitement about a special event or simply having outgrown the need for a daytime sleep. Most under-fours need to lie down and relax during the day, but children older than this usually will not need a daytime sleep. You should still aim to create a restful mood at some point in the day for the older child, by reading quietly, playing soothing music or doing quiet activities, such as completing a jigsaw.

Bedtime routines

Depending on the hours you work, you may well be involved in young children's bedtime routines. For example, as a live-in nanny caring for a young child whose usual bedtime is 7.30 p.m., but whose parents do not get back from work until 8.30 p.m. on some nights, you may be responsible for carrying out the entire bedtime routine for the child. Some parents may want you to bath the child and get them ready for bed, but prefer to put the child to bed themselves so that they can share a special time with their child to talk about the child's day, read stories and/or sing songs. Even if you work as a daily nanny, you will still have some babysitting duties and this will often include bathing and putting the child to bed.

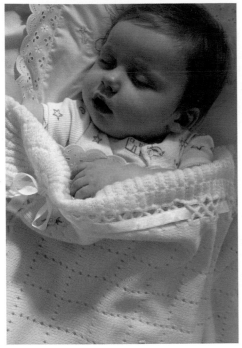
Baby having a nap

You will need to follow any parental instructions regarding the child's bedtime routine. If the child already has an established bedtime routine, you should follow that. Sometimes the parents of a baby or very young child may want your help to establish a regular bedtime routine. Bedtime routines are an important part of a child's sleeping habits. A consistent and short bedtime routine lets the child know that bedtime is approaching and it also helps to relax them for bed. The bedtime routine needs to be carried out at the same time each evening and should be similar each night. Ensure the bedtime routine is a pleasurable experience by giving the child plenty of time and attention.

A typical bedtime routine could be:

❋ play a quiet game
❋ bath or wash, put on pyjamas and brush teeth
❋ use the potty or toilet (whichever is appropriate)
❋ say goodnight to everyone and get into bed
❋ have a chat about the day's events
❋ parent/nanny reads a short story
❋ tuck the child in and say goodnight
❋ parent/nanny leaves the room and the child settles to sleep.

Bath-time

Although some parents like their babies to have a bath every day, until the baby is crawling around and getting into things, a bath is really only necessary once or twice a week. (Just wash their face/hands frequently and thoroughly clean the genital and anal areas after each nappy change.) Most babies and young children find bath-time very soothing and relaxing. If the baby or child really enjoys the bath-time routine (and the parents wish it), you can give the child a daily bath.

Bath-time can be fun for you and the child, but you must always remember safety. (There is more information about bath-time safety in the next section.)

EXERCISE: Outline a daily routine for a baby or young child.

MAINTAINING CHILDREN'S SAFETY

Make sure you know about basic first aid, especially for babies and young children (see chapter 2). Make sure you know if the parents are expecting anyone to call at the house when they are out at work. Remember that you should not allow anyone into the house unless they produce proper and verifiable identification and have a valid purpose for entering the house, e.g. gas and electricity employees or the emergency services. To maintain young children's safety you must always keep a close watch over them in the home and garden, in the car, and when out and about.

Children's safety in the home and garden

One of the biggest threats to children's safety and security is in their own home. Over 40 per cent of accidents involving children occur at home or in the garden. Those most at risk from home accidents are children under five; in 2002 almost 480,000 children accidentally injured in the home were under five years old (Child Accident Prevention Trust 2002a).

It is important when caring for young children that you know the potential risks children face as they develop and learn new skills.

You can help to prevent injuries to young children by:

❊ never leaving a baby unattended on a changing table (or other furniture)
❊ using safety gates fitted at the top and bottom of the stairs
❊ encouraging children to put away their toys after use
❊ keeping matches and lighters out of the sight and reach of children
❊ using fireguards on all fires and heaters
❊ keeping young children away from cookers, ovens and hobs

* using short flexes with kettles and keeping them out of children's reach
* keeping mugs/cups of hot drinks away from children – never hold a child while you are drinking a hot drink
* never doing the ironing with the children around – do it when they are asleep or at nursery/school – and remember to turn off the iron after use
* keeping all medicines out of the sight and reach of children – ideally in a locked cabinet or cupboard
* keeping dangerous substances in their original containers and out of the reach of children, including bleach, detergents, cleaners, paints, thinners, varnishes and glues
* keeping perfumes, nail varnishes, essential oils and alcohol out of children's reach
* supervising children in or near water at all times
* never leaving a young child in the bath alone (see bath-time safety below)
* ensuring that garden ponds are either drained or securely covered
* marking large areas of glass with large stickers, e.g. patio doors
* ensuring child-proof safety catches are fitted on drawers containing sharp knives etc.
* keeping small objects such as coins and toy parts away from young children
* keeping plastic bags and cling film out of children's reach
* following the age recommendations on toys and outdoor play equipment.

(Child Accident Prevention Trust 2002a)

Bath-time safety

Always remember these important bath-time safety rules:

1   Never leave the child unsupervised, even for a minute. Children can drown in less than an inch of water in less than 60 seconds. If someone knocks at the door or the phone rings, ignore it – if it is important they will call back.

2   Never put the child into a bath when the water is still running, as the water temperature could change or the depth could become too high.

3   Make the bath safe by putting in a rubber bathmat and covering the taps.

4   Make sure the bath water is comfortably warm (about 32–35°C). Children generally prefer a much cooler bath than adults.

5   Fill the bath with only 5–7.5 centimetres (2–3 inches) of water for babies up to six months old, and never more than waist-high (in a sitting position) for older children.

6   Teach the child to sit in the bath at all times.

7   Do not allow the child to touch the taps. Even if they cannot turn them on now, they will be strong enough to do so soon and that could lead to serious injury. In any case, a hot tap may burn the child even without the water running.

Toy safety

Every year in the UK over 35,000 children under the age of 15 years are treated in hospital following an accident involving a toy. Most of these accidents involve children aged one to three years (Child Accident Prevention Trust 2002b).

It is essential to provide babies and young children with toys that are appropriate for their age and level of development. Most toys will have a suggested age range. However, some toys will have a warning to indicate that the toy is unsuitable for children under 36 months as it may contain parts that could be a choking hazard for a baby or very young child. It is a legal requirement for all toys sold in the European Union to carry a CE mark, but this does not necessarily guarantee safety or quality. When selecting toys for young children always look for one of these safety marks:

❋ European Standard BS EN 71 to show that the toy has been tested to the agreed safety standards

❋ The Lion Mark to show that the toy has been made to the highest standards of safety and quality.

Children's safety in the car

As a nanny you may be required to transport the child (or children) in your care in the family car or your own car. The main safety requirement when transporting a young child in a car is that an appropriate car seat is installed and used correctly. Other safety issues include having child locks to prevent the child from getting out of the car should they manage to undo the child restraint. Always remember that you should never leave a child unattended in a parked car – a young child could die in hot weather or be abducted by a stranger.

Children's safety when out and about

You must always tell the parents about any planned activities or outings so they know where you and the child are at all times. Always have your mobile telephone with you when out and about so that you can contact someone in an emergency. Always have the telephone numbers of the parents and one of their close friends or relatives you can contact if the parents are unavailable. Make sure the parents have your mobile telephone number so they can contact you if necessary.

You must never leave a baby or young child in a pram/pushchair outside a shop or let a toddler wander off. You should always use a five-point safety harness to secure the child in a pram or pushchair to prevent them falling out. When out walking or shopping with a young child you should always use a five-point safety harness to prevent them running off, especially near busy roads or water.

Out and about with a toddler

When visiting other people's homes or when on holiday with the family, remember to maintain the children's safety by checking that medicines and other potentially dangerous substances are out of their reach. Remember that not everyone may be as safety-conscious as you and that other houses (or holiday accommodation) may not be organized with crawling babies or inquisitive toddlers in mind.

(For more information about outings, travelling with children and holidays, see chapter 11.)

FIRST AID

First aid is the care given to a casualty before professional medical assistance arrives. The help that you give to a baby or young child who is injured or seriously ill can literally mean the difference between life and death.

The aims of first aid

1 To preserve life by:
- providing emergency resuscitation
- controlling bleeding
- treating burns
- treating shock.

2   To prevent the worsening of any injuries by:
  ❋ covering wounds
  ❋ immobilizing fractures
  ❋ placing the casualty in the correct and comfortable position.

3   To promote recovery by:
  ❋ providing reassurance
  ❋ giving any other treatment needed
  ❋ relieving pain
  ❋ handling gently
  ❋ moving as little as possible
  ❋ protecting from the cold.

The priorities of first aid

❋ A is for Airway: establish an open airway by tilting the forehead back so that the child can breathe easily.
❋ B is for Breathing: check that the child is breathing by listening, looking and feeling for breath.
❋ C is for Circulation: apply simple visual checks that the child's blood is circulating adequately, by watching for improved colour, coughing or eye movement.

What to do in a medical emergency

Knowing what to do if a child has an accident is extremely important. In a serious accident or other emergency, prompt action could save the child's life. Always make sure that your first aid training is up-to-date.

Always keep a note of essential telephone numbers in a convenient place. This includes the telephone numbers of the parents, the child's GP and relatives, family friends or neighbours who can be contacted quickly. You should also have the numbers and addresses of hospitals with accident and emergency (A&E) departments, in case you need to take the child to hospital.

If you think the child may have severe injuries or a serious illness, dial 999 for an ambulance or take the child to a hospital A&E department. However, there are times when the most urgent need is for immediate first aid, as in the case of severe bleeding, choking and breathing difficulties.

Remember these important points:

1   Keep calm. Remaining calm will help the child to keep calm and cooperate. If the child becomes anxious or excited the extent of the damage from the injury could be increased.

2   Plan quickly what needs to be done. Learn basic first aid procedures and/or have your first aid manual handy.

3   Send for medical assistance. Reaching help quickly could save the child's life. Know your local emergency telephone numbers.

4   Provide reassurance to the child. Let the child know that help is on the way and try to make them as comfortable as possible.

> **EXERCISE:** Describe what you would do in a medical emergency involving a young child in the family home.

First aid kit

Some ready-assembled first aid kits are economical and include most of the items you will find essential for giving first aid. If you cannot find everything you need in one first aid kit, start with a pre-packaged kit and then add any extra items you require. Remember you will also need to keep many of these items locked in the family medicine cupboard.

Here are some suggestions for the contents of a first-aid kit:

* a first aid manual or first aid leaflet
* an assortment of sticky plasters in various sizes and shapes
* assorted bandages, including a wrapped triangular bandage, a one-inch and a two-inch strip for holding dressings and compresses in place
* medium and large individually wrapped sterile unmedicated wound dressings
* two sterile eye pads
* safety pins
* adhesive tape
* sterile gauze
* a pair of sharp scissors
* tweezers and needles for splinters and thorns
* one pair of disposable gloves
* child thermometer
* children's liquid pain reliever (do not use aspirin; use paracetamol in liquid form; always give doses as recommended by the child's doctor)
* an oral syringe or calibrated cup or spoon for administering medicines to children
* antibacterial cream for cuts and scrapes
* children's insect repellent and sting reliever spray for insect bites
* children's sunscreen lotion
* calamine lotion for sunburn and rashes
* if the child has asthma or is allergic to bee stings, peanuts, shellfish or has any type of life-threatening allergy, remember to carry their medication with you at all times and keep spare medication in the first aid kit.

As well as a large first aid kit for the family home, it is a good idea to have a mini first aid kit for your handbag, rucksack or nappy-changing bag for when you are out and about. Remember to store the first aid kit in a bag that can be fastened securely and kept out of reach of babies and children, as any item in a first aid kit can be dangerous to a young child.

COMMON CHILDHOOD ILLNESSES AND HEALTH PROBLEMS

Babies and young children should be vaccinated against diseases, including diphtheria, measles, meningitis, mumps, polio, rubella, tetanus and whooping cough. The first immunizations start when a baby is two months old. The child's parents will usually receive appointments by post to attend their local clinic or GP surgery. It may be your responsibility to take the child for these immunizations, especially if the parents are at work.

As a nanny you need to be aware of the range of illnesses and health problems that may affect babies and young children. These include: allergies, asthma, chicken pox, colds, coughs, diabetes, diarrhoea, earache, eczema, epilepsy, flu, headache, sore throat, toothache, vomiting.

Recognizing signs and symptoms

By knowing the usual behaviour and appearance of the young child or children you work with, you will be able to recognize any significant changes that might indicate possible ill health. You need to be able to recognize the differences between young children who are pretending to be ill, feeling 'under the weather', experiencing a common illness or experiencing a more serious health problem.

The signs of possible ill health in young children include:

✳ changes in facial colour (e.g. becoming pale or very red)

✳ changes in temperature (e.g. becoming very hot or cold, becoming clammy or shivering – a fever usually indicates that the child has an infection)

✳ changes in behaviour (e.g. not wanting to play when would usually be very keen)

✳ being upset or generally distressed

✳ having reduced concentration levels or falling asleep more often than usual

✳ scratching excessively

✳ complaining of persistent pain (e.g. headache or stomach-ache)

✳ coughing or sneezing excessively

✳ diarrhoea and/or vomiting

✳ displaying a rash (this could indicate an infection or allergic reaction; make sure you know if the child has severe allergic reactions).

(Watkinson 2003)

Responding to signs and symptoms

You should know what to do if a young child experiences ill health while in your care. The most common childhood illness in young children is the common cold. A young child may have as many as five or six colds a year. Colds and flu are caused by viruses and so cannot be helped by antibiotics. However, cold and flu viruses can weaken the body and lead to a secondary bacterial infection such as tonsillitis, otitis media (middle ear infection), sinusitis, bronchitis and pneumonia. These bacterial infections require antibiotic treatment.

You should seek medical advice if you have concerns about any of the following:

❉ the child's high temperature lasts for more than 24 hours
❉ the child has a persistent cough with green or yellow catarrh (possible bronchitis or pneumonia)
❉ the child has pain above the eyes or in the face (possible sinusitis)
❉ the child has a severe sore throat (possible tonsillitis)
❉ the child has a bad earache (possible ear infection).

Seek medical advice immediately if:

❉ a baby under 6 months has a temperature of more than 37°C
❉ you think the child may have meningitis
❉ the child has breathing difficulties
❉ the child's asthma deteriorates
❉ the child has a convulsion
❉ the child has very poor fluid intake or cannot swallow liquids
❉ a baby persistently refuses to take feeds
❉ in the last 12 months the child has been to a country where there is a risk of malaria.

Caring for sick children

Give verbal reassurance to a child who is feeling unwell or just miserable. A baby or very young child may seek physical comfort such as a cuddle or sitting on your lap. You may need to provide additional opportunities for rest and sleep. Get the child to rest and avoid vigorous play or exercise. Ensure you make the child as comfortable as possible. Encourage the child to drink plenty of fluids even if they do not have much of an appetite. Provide soothing and relaxing activities appropriate to the child's age/level of development and degree of illness, such as playing quiet music, reading stories, singing songs and rhymes, providing colouring activities, doing jigsaws and simple games.

When caring for sick children you should always remember to:

❉ ensure that you know what to do when a child is seriously ill or injured
❉ summon assistance for any medical emergency (see first aid above)
❉ report any concerns about health problems to the child's parents.

CHILD PROTECTION

Information on child protection issues can be found in the guidance document *Working Together To Safeguard Children*, prepared and issued jointly by the Department of Health, the Home Office and the Department for Education in 1999. This replaces *Working Together Under the Children Act 1989*, published in 1991. This new guidance is still informed by the requirements of the Children Act 1989, which provides a comprehensive framework for the care and protection of children. The guidance also echoes the principles covered by the United Nations Convention on the Rights of the Child, endorsed by the UK government in 1991. It also takes on board the European Convention of Human Rights, especially Articles 6 and 8. All adults who work with children (including nannies) have a duty to safeguard and promote the welfare of children.

Defining child abuse

The Children Act 1989 defines child abuse as a person's actions that cause a child to suffer significant harm to their health, development or well-being.
   Significant harm can be caused by:

※ punishing a child too much

※ hitting or shaking a child

※ constantly criticizing, threatening or rejecting a child

※ sexually interfering with or assaulting a child

※ neglecting a child, e.g. not giving them enough to eat or not ensuring their safety.

When child abuse happens, the perpetrator is usually someone in the child's immediate family circle. This may be a parent, brother, sister, babysitter or other familiar adult. It is very unusual for strangers to be involved in most cases of child abuse (Royal College of Psychiatrists 2002).

Recognizing the signs and symptoms of abuse or neglect

As a nanny, you need to be aware of the signs and symptoms of possible child abuse and neglect and know to whom you should report any concerns or suspicions. As a nanny you have contact with a child on a day-to-day basis and so have an essential role to play in detecting indicators of possible abuse or neglect: outward signs of physical abuse, uncharacteristic behaviour patterns or failure to develop in the expected ways.

Possible signs and symptoms of physical abuse include:

* recurrent unexplained injuries or burns
* refusal to discuss injuries
* improbable explanations for injuries
* watchful, cautious attitude towards adults
* reluctance to play and be spontaneous
* shrinking from physical contact
* avoidance of activities involving removal of clothes
* aggressive or bullying behaviour
* being bullied
* lack of concentration
* deterioration of school work
* lying, stealing or truanting from school
* difficulty in trusting people and making friends.

Possible signs and symptoms of sexual abuse include:

* sudden behaviour changes when abuse begins
* low self-esteem
* using sexual words or ideas in play activities that are uncharacteristic for age/level of development
* withdrawn or secretive behaviour
* deterioration in school work
* starting to wet or soil themselves
* sleep problems, e.g. insomnia or nightmares
* demonstrate inappropriate seductive or flirtatious behaviour
* frequent public masturbation
* frightened of physical contact
* depression resulting in self-harm or an overdose
* running away from home
* bruises, scratches, burns or bite marks on the body
* persistent infections in the anal or genital areas.

Possible signs and symptoms of emotional abuse include:

* delayed speech development
* very passive and lacking in spontaneity
* social isolation, e.g. finding it hard to develop close relationships
* unable to engage in imaginative play
* low self-esteem
* easily distracted

* poor academic performance at school
* fear of new situations
* self-damaging behaviour, e.g. head-banging, pulling out hair
* self-absorbing behaviour, e.g. obsessive rocking, thumb sucking
* eating problems, e.g. overeating or lack of appetite
* withdrawn behaviour and depression.

Possible signs and symptoms of neglect include:

* slow physical development
* constant hunger and/or tiredness
* poor personal hygiene and appearance
* frequent lateness or absenteeism
* undiagnosed/untreated medical conditions
* social isolation, e.g. poor social relationships
* compulsive stealing or begging.

(Royal College of Psychiatrists 2002)

Personal disclosures

If a child makes a personal disclosure that they have been abused in some way, you should:

* listen to what the child has to say
* accept what the child is saying
* allow the child to talk openly
* listen to the child rather than ask direct questions
* not criticize the alleged perpetrator of the abuse
* reassure the child that what has happened is not their fault
* stress to the child that it was the right thing to tell someone
* reassure the child but not make promises that you might not be able to keep
* not promise the child to keep the disclosed information confidential (as it might be necessary for the matter to be to referred to social services or the police)
* explain simply to the child what has to be done next and who has to be told.

After the child has made a disclosure to you:

* make brief notes as soon as possible after the conversation
* do not destroy the original notes, as the courts may need these
* record the date, time, place and any noticeable non-verbal behaviour and the words used by the child
* draw a diagram to indicate the position of any bruising or other injury
* record only statements and observations rather than interpretations or assumptions.

Dealing with a disclosure from a child or being involved in a child protection case is usually a very stressful experience. You may require support for yourself and should discuss this in confidence with someone you trust, e.g. your GP.

Reporting concerns

If you think that a child in your care is at risk from abuse or neglect, you must pass on this information to an appropriate person, e.g. your local social services department, the NSPCC or the police, and tell them about your concerns. If you are in any doubt, you should talk to a person with experience of working with children who can advise you about what to do next, e.g. talk to your GP first without revealing the identity of the child.

Further reading

Burney, L., 1999, *Optimum Nutrition for Babies and Young Children*, Piatkus Books.

Dare, A. and O'Donovan, M., 2000, *Good Practice in Child Safety*, Nelson Thornes.

Dare, A. and O'Donovan, M., 2002, *A Practical Guide to Child Nutrition*, 2nd edition, Nelson Thornes.

Department of Health, the Home Office and the Department for Education, 1999, *Working Together to Safeguard Children*, HMSO.

Hobart, C. and Frankel, J., 1998, *Good Practice in Child Protection*, Nelson Thornes.

Kay, J., 2003, *Protecting Children*, Continuum International Publishing.

Lindon, J., 2003, *Child Protection*, 2nd edition, Hodder and Stoughton.

Meggitt, C., 1999, *Caring for Babies*, Hodder and Stoughton.

Paterson, G., 2002, Foreword, *First Aid For Children Fast*, Dorling Kindersley in association with The British Red Cross.

Rowley, B., 2000, *Baby Days: activities, ideas, and games for enjoying daily life with a child under three*, Hyperion Books.

Stoppard, M., 2001, *Complete Baby and Childcare*, Dorling Kindersley.

Valman, B., 2002, *BMA When Your Child is Ill: a home guide for parents*, Dorling Kindersley.

Woolfson, R., 1997, *The Professional Nanny Handbook, Nursery World* edition, Caring Books.

Child development and early learning **8**

* Understanding all aspects of young children's development
* Young children's physical development
* Young children's language development
* Young children's intellectual development
* Early learning
* Developing children's early literacy skills
* Developing children's early numeracy skills

UNDERSTANDING ALL ASPECTS OF YOUNG CHILDREN'S DEVELOPMENT

All children are special and unique; *all* children have individual needs because they perceive the world differently and interact with other people in different ways. *All* children have these essential needs:

* **p**hysical care: regular, nutritious meals, warmth, rest and sleep
* **r**outines: a regular pattern to their day, with any changes explained
* **i**ndependence: encouragement to do things for themselves and make choices
* **c**ommunication: encouragement to talk and interact with others
* **e**ncouragement and praise: for effort as well as achievement
* **l**ove: which is unconditional, from parents and carers
* **e**ducation: appropriate to their ages and levels of development
* **s**incerity and respect: honest and courteous treatment
* **s**timulation: exploring their environment and tackling new challenges.

When looking at young children's development and early learning it is important to use a holistic approach. You should remember to look at the whole child. When planning learning activities and experiences for young children you should consider all aspects of their development:

* **s**ocial
* **p**hysical
* **i**ntellectual
* **c**ommunication (language)
* **e**motional.

(This chapter deals with physical, intellectual and communication skills. Chapter 9 looks at social and emotional skills, including managing young children's behaviour. Chapter 10 looks at play and planning early learning activities.)

The sequence of young children's development

It is more accurate to think in terms of a sequence of children's development rather than stages of development. This is because stages refer to development that occurs at *fixed ages*, while sequence indicates development that follows the same basic pattern, *but not necessarily at fixed ages*.

You should really use the term 'sequence' when referring to all aspects of young children's development. However, the work of people such as Mary Sheridan provides a useful guide to the milestones of *expected* development, that is, the usual pattern of children's development (or norm). As well as being affected by their chronological age, children's development is affected by many other factors, e.g. social interaction, play opportunities, early learning experiences, special needs.

The developmental charts in this book do indicate specific ages, but only to provide a framework to help you understand young children's development. You should always remember that all children are unique individuals and develop at their own rate.

YOUNG CHILDREN'S PHYSICAL DEVELOPMENT

Physical development involves children's increasing ability to perform more complex physical activities, involving gross motor skills, fine motor skills and coordination.

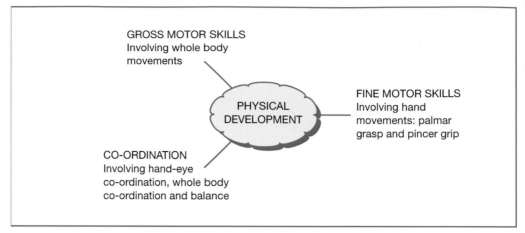

Gross motor skills

Gross motor skills involve whole body movements. Examples of gross motor skills include rolling over, crawling, walking, running, climbing stairs, hopping, jumping, skipping, riding a tricycle/bicycle, swimming, climbing play apparatus, throwing and catching a ball, playing football, somersaults, handstands, cartwheels. Children need strength, stamina and suppleness to become proficient in activities involving gross motor skills.

Fine motor skills

Fine motor skills involve whole hand movements, wrist action or delicate procedures using the fingers, e.g. the palmar grasp (grabbing and holding a small brick), the pincer grip (using the thumb and index finger to pick up a pea), tripod grasp (holding a crayon, pencil or pen). Examples of fine motor skills include drawing, painting, writing, model-making, playing with wooden/plastic bricks or construction kits, cutting with scissors, doing up/undoing buttons, shoelaces and other fastenings. Children need good concentration levels and hand-eye coordination (see below) to become proficient in activities involving fine motor skills.

Coordination

Coordination involves hand-eye coordination, whole body coordination and balance. Examples of hand-eye coordination include drawing, painting, using scissors, writing and threading beads. Examples of whole body coordination include crawling, walking, cycling, swimming and playing football. Examples of balance include hopping and gymnastics. Coordination plays an important part in developing children's gross and fine motor skills. Coordination and balance are needed to improve children's gross motor skills. Precise hand or finger movements involve the use of the eyes in coordination with the hands, e.g. hand-eye coordination.

You should provide appropriate opportunities for young children to develop their physical skills (see below). Remember that some children may be limited in their physical abilities due to physical disability, sensory impairment or other special needs.

The sequence of physical development: 0–8 years

Age 0–3 months

* sleeps much of the time and grows fast
* tries to lift head
* starts to kick legs, with movements gradually becoming smoother
* starts to wave arms about
* begins to hold objects when placed in hand, e.g. an appropriate size/shaped rattle
* grasp reflex diminishes as hand and eye coordination begins to develop
* enjoys finger play (e.g. simple finger rhymes)
* becomes more alert when awake
* learns to roll from side on to back
* sees best at distance of 25 cm, then gradually starts watching objects further away
* needs opportunities to play and exercise (e.g. soft toys, cloth books and playmat with different textures and sounds).

Age 3–9 months

* establishes head control – moves head round to follow people and objects
* begins to sit with support – from about 6 months sits unsupported
* rolls over
* may begin to crawl, stand and cruise while holding on to furniture (from about six months)
* learns to pull self up to sitting position
* begins to use palmar grasp and transfers objects from one hand to the other
* develops pincer grasp using thumb and index finger from about six months
* continues to enjoy finger rhymes
* drops things deliberately and searches for hidden/dropped objects (from about eight months)
* puts objects into containers and takes them out
* enjoys water play in the bath
* needs opportunities for play and exercise including soft toys, board books, bricks, containers, activity centres.

Age 9–18 months

* is now very mobile (e.g. crawls, bottom-shuffles, cruises, walks)
* starts to go upstairs (with supervision), but has difficulty coming down

* needs safe environment in which to explore as becomes increasingly mobile (e.g. remember safety gates on stairs)
* throws toys deliberately
* watches ball rolling towards self and tries to push it back
* has mature pincer grasp and can scribble with crayons
* points to objects using index finger
* places one (or more) bricks on top of each other to make a small tower
* holds a cup and tries to feed self
* continues to enjoy finger rhymes plus simple action songs.

Age 18 months–2 years

* starts using potty but has difficulty keeping dry
* can feed self
* walks well and tries to run but has difficulty stopping
* comes downstairs on front with help
* learns to push a pedal-less tricycle or sit-and-ride toy with feet
* tries to throw ball but has difficulty catching
* bends down to pick things up
* uses several bricks to make a tower
* as fine motor skills improve, continues to scribble and can do very simple jigsaw puzzles
* enjoys action songs and rhymes
* needs space, materials and opportunities to play alongside other children.

Age 2–3 years

* uses potty and stays dry more reliably
* comes downstairs in upright position one stair at a time
* starts to climb well on play apparatus
* kicks a ball, learns to jump and may learn to somersault
* learns to pedal a tricycle
* can undress self; tries to dress self, but needs help, especially with socks and fastenings
* fine motor skills improving – has increased control of crayons and paintbrush, tries to use scissors
* enjoys construction activities and can build more complex structures
* continues to enjoy action songs and rhymes
* needs space, materials and opportunities to play alongside and with other children.

Age 3–4 years

* usually clean and dry but may have occasional 'accidents'
* able to run well – and stop!

- ✳ competent at gross motor skills such as jumping, riding a tricycle, climbing play apparatus, using a swing
- ✳ throws and catches a ball, but is still inaccurate
- ✳ fine motor skills continue to improve, e.g. can use scissors
- ✳ continues to enjoy action songs plus simple singing and dancing games
- ✳ needs space, materials and opportunities to play cooperatively with other children.

Age 4–5 years

- ✳ clean and dry but may still have occasional 'accidents' if absorbed in an activity or upset
- ✳ can dress/undress self, but may still need help with intricate fastenings and shoelaces
- ✳ has improved gross motor skills and coordination, so is more proficient at running, jumping, climbing and balancing
- ✳ has some difficulty with hopping and skipping
- ✳ has improved ball skills but still learning to use a bat
- ✳ may learn to ride a bicycle (with stabilizers)
- ✳ enjoys swimming activities
- ✳ fine motor skills continue to improve: has better pencil/crayon control; is more competent at handling materials and making things
- ✳ continues to enjoy action songs plus singing and dancing games
- ✳ needs space, materials and opportunities to play cooperatively with other children.

Age 5–8 years

- ✳ clean and dry but may very rarely have an 'accident' if absorbed in an activity or very upset
- ✳ can dress/undress self, including fastenings and shoelaces
- ✳ grows taller and thinner, starts losing baby teeth
- ✳ improved gross motor skills and coordination lead to proficiency in climbing, running, jumping, balancing, hopping and skipping
- ✳ can hit a ball with a bat
- ✳ learns to ride a bicycle (without stabilizers)
- ✳ learns to swim (if taught properly)
- ✳ as fine motor skills improve, handwriting becomes easier and more legible
- ✳ can do more complex construction activities
- ✳ continues to enjoy singing and dancing games
- ✳ needs space, materials and opportunities to engage in more complex cooperative activities with other children.

Baby playing with activity centre

Ten ways to promote a young child's physical skills

1 Select activities, tools and materials that are appropriate to the age and level of development of the child.

2 Provide opportunities for the child to explore and experiment with their physical skills both indoors and outdoors, with and without play apparatus or other equipment.

3 Maintain the child's safety by supervising the child at all times and checking that any equipment used meets required safety standards and is positioned on an appropriate surface. Ensure the child knows how to use any equipment correctly and safely.

4 Provide opportunities for the child to repeat actions until they are confident and competent. Provide specific tools and activities to help the child practise their physical skills. Encourage child to persevere with tackling a new skill that is particularly difficult by reassuring the child that everyone needs practice and patience to learn new skills.

5 Use everyday routines to develop the child's fine motor skills, e.g. getting dressed, dealing with fastenings and shoelaces, using a cup, using a spoon, fork or knife, helping prepare or serve food, setting the table, washing up (remember safety).

6 Provide play opportunities to help the child practise fine motor skills, e.g. bricks, jigsaws, playdough, sand, construction kits, drawing.

7   Help the child to develop body awareness through action songs such as 'Head, shoulders, knees and toes'.

8   Encourage and praise the child as they become competent in each physical skill.

9   Allow the child to be as independent as possible when developing physical skills.

10 Adapt activities and/or use specialist equipment for a child with special needs to enable their participation in physical activities as appropriate.

YOUNG CHILDREN'S LANGUAGE DEVELOPMENT

Language is the key factor in all children's development as it provides them with the skills they need to communicate with others, relate to others, explore the environment, understand concepts, formulate ideas and express feelings.

Young children (and adults) use a variety of different ways to communicate. These modes of language are essential to being able to communicate effectively with others and being fully involved in a wide range of social interactions.

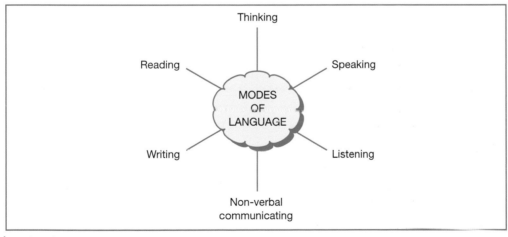

Modes of language

You should provide opportunities for young children to develop the necessary skills to become competent at communicating using these different modes of language. Opportunities for talk are especially helpful in promoting the development and use of language. When working with young children, you must be aware of and provide for appropriate experiences to enable the children to develop effective communication skills.

The sequence of language development: 0–8 years

Age 0–3 months

* recognizes familiar voices, stops crying when hears them
* aware of other sounds, turns head towards sounds
* responds to smiles
* moves whole body in response to sound/to attract attention
* pauses to listen to others
* makes noises as well as crying (e.g. burbling).

Age 3–9 months

* responds with smiles
* recognizes family names but cannot say them
* enjoys looking at pictures and books
* even more responsive to voices and music
* participates in simple games (e.g. 'peep-po')
* tries to imitate sounds (e.g. during rhymes)
* starts babbling, uses single syllable sounds (e.g. 'daa', 'baa' and 'maa')
* from about seven months uses two-syllable sounds (e.g. 'daada', 'baaba', 'maama')
* shouts to attract attention.

Age 9–18 months

* continues to imitate sounds
* starts jargoning (e.g. joins up syllables so more like sentences, such as 'Maama-baaba-daa')
* learns to say first real words, usually the names of animals and everyday things
* uses gestures to emphasize word meanings
* uses vocabulary of 3–20 words
* participates in simple finger rhymes
* continues to enjoy books
* overextends words, that is, uses same word to identify similar objects (e.g. all round objects are called 'ball').

Age 18 months–2 years

* uses language to gain information (e.g. starts asking 'What dat?')
* repeats words said by adults
* acquires one to three words per month; by two years has vocabulary of about 200 words
* participates in action songs and nursery rhymes
* continues to enjoy books and stories
* uses telegraphic speech (e.g. speaks in two- to three-word sentences, such as 'Daddy go' or 'Milk all gone').

Age 2–3 years

* has vocabulary of about 300 words
* uses more adult forms of speech (e.g. sentences now include words like 'that', 'this', 'here', 'there', 'then', 'but', 'and')
* can name main body parts
* uses adjectives such as 'big', 'small', 'tall'
* uses words referring to relationships (e.g. 'I', 'my', 'you', 'yours')
* asks questions to gain more information
* sings songs and rhymes, continues to participate in action songs
* continues to enjoy books and stories
* can deliver simple messages.

Age 3–4 years

* has vocabulary of 900–1000 words
* asks lots of questions
* uses language to ask for assistance
* talks constantly to people knows well
* gives very simple accounts of past events
* can say names of colours
* begins to vocalize ideas
* continues to enjoy books, stories, songs and rhymes
* listens to and can follow simple instructions
* can deliver verbal messages.

Age 4–5 years

* may use vocabulary of about 1500–2000 words
* uses more complex sentence structures
* asks even more questions, using 'what', 'when', 'who', 'where', 'how' and especially 'why'!
* shows interest in more complex books and stories
* gives more detailed accounts of past events
* vocalizes ideas and feelings
* can listen to and follow more detailed instructions
* can deliver more complex verbal messages
* continues to enjoy songs and rhymes
* shows interest in simple poetry.

Age 5–8 years

* has extensive vocabulary; by eight years may use as many as 5000 words
* uses more complex sentence structures
* develops early reading skills

* develops early writing skills, but possibly at slower rate than reading skills
* continues to enjoy books, stories and poetry (by age seven can recall the story so far if book read a chapter at a time)
* gives very detailed accounts of past events and can anticipate future events
* vocalizes ideas and feelings in more depth
* listens to and follows more complex instructions
* appreciates simple jokes due to more sophisticated language knowledge
* uses developing literacy skills to communicate and to access information (e.g. story and letter writing, use of dictionaries, encyclopaedias, computers, Internet, email).

Adult talking with young child

Ten ways to encourage a young child's language/communication skills

1 Talk to the baby or young child about anything and everything!
2 Show the child what you are talking about (e.g. use real objects/situations, pictures, books and other visual or audio aids).
3 Use straightforward sentences with words appropriate to the child's level of understanding and development; avoid oversimplifying language; do not use 'baby talk' – the child needs to hear adult speech to learn language.
4 Use repetition to introduce/reinforce new vocabulary and ideas; do not make the child repeat things over and over – this is boring and frustrating.

5 Copy the child's sounds/words, including any extensions or corrections, to reinforce positively and extend the child's vocabulary, sentence structures etc. (e.g. if the child says 'Ball', you could reply, 'Yes, that is Tom's red ball'; or if the child says 'Moo!', you could reply, 'Yes, the cow goes "moo"!'); never tell children off for making language errors – it will only make them reluctant to communicate in the future (making mistakes is part of the language learning process).

6 Be lively! Use your tone of voice and facial expressions to convey your interest in what is being communicated.

7 Remember turn-taking in language exchanges – ask questions to stimulate the child's responses and to encourage speech.

8 Look at the child when you are talking with them – remember to be at the child's level, e.g. sit on a low chair or even on the floor (do *not* tower over them).

9 Let the child initiate conversations and listen to what they have to say.

10 Share books, stories and rhymes with young children, including babies.

YOUNG CHILDREN'S INTELLECTUAL DEVELOPMENT

Intellectual or cognitive development involves the process of gaining, storing, recalling and using information. The interrelated components of intellectual development are: thinking, perception, language, problem-solving, concepts, memory, concentration and creativity.

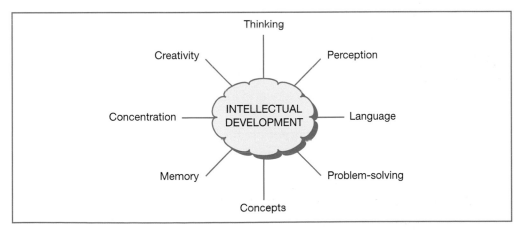

Intellectual development

To develop as healthy, considerate and intelligent human beings, babies and young children require intellectual stimulation as well as physical care and emotional security. Babies and young children are constantly thinking and learning, gathering new information and formulating new ideas about themselves, other people and the world around them.

The sequence of intellectual development: 0–8 years

Age 0–3 months

* recognizes parents
* concentrates on familiar voices rather than unfamiliar ones
* aware of different smells
* explores by putting objects in mouth
* observes objects that move
* responds to bright colours and bold images
* stores and recalls information through images
* sees everything in relation to self (is egocentric).

Age 3–9 months

* knows individuals and recognizes familiar faces
* recognizes certain sounds and objects
* shows interest in everything, especially toys and books
* concentrates on well-defined objects and follows direction of moving object
* anticipates familiar actions and enjoys games, such as 'peep-po'
* searches for hidden or dropped objects (from about eight months)
* observes what happens at home and when out and about
* explores immediate environment once mobile
* processes information through images
* enjoys water play in the bath
* sees everything in relation to self (is still egocentric).

Age 9–18 months

* explores immediate environment using senses (especially sight and touch), has no sense of danger
* concentrates more, due to curiosity and increased physical skills, but still has short attention span
* follows one-step instructions and/or gestured commands
* observes other people closely and tries to imitate their actions
* uses trial-and-error methods when playing with bricks, containers
* searches for hidden or dropped objects (aware of object permanence)
* learns that objects can be grouped together
* continues to store and recall information through images
* is still egocentric.

Age 18 months–2 years

* recognizes objects from pictures and books
* points to desired objects, selects named objects

* matches basic colours, starts to match shapes
* does very simple puzzles
* follows one-step instructions
* concentrates for longer (e.g. searching for hidden object), but attention span still quite short
* shows lots of curiosity and continues exploring using senses and trial-and-error methods
* processes information through images and, increasingly, through language
* shows preferences and starts to make choices
* is still egocentric.

Age 2–3 years

* identifies facial features and main body parts
* continues to imitate other children and adults
* follows two-step instructions
* matches more colours and shapes, including puzzles and other matching activities
* points to named objects in pictures and books
* develops understanding of big and small
* begins to understand concept of time at basic level (e.g. before/after, today/tomorrow)
* enjoys imaginative play, able to use symbols in play (e.g. pretend a doll is a real baby)
* concentrates on intricate tasks such as creative activities or construction, but may still have short attention span, especially if not really interested in the activity
* is very preoccupied with own activities – still egocentric
* shows some awareness of right and wrong
* processes information through language rather than images.

Age 3–4 years

* learns about basic concepts through play
* experiments with colour, shape and texture
* recalls a simple sequence of events
* follows two- or three-step instructions, including positional ones (e.g. 'Please put your ball in the box under the table')
* continues to enjoy imaginative and creative play
* interested in more complex construction activities
* concentrates on more complex activities as attention span increases
* plays cooperatively with other children, able to accept and share ideas in group activities

* shows some awareness of right and wrong, the needs of others
* holds strong opinions about likes and dislikes
* processes information using language.

Age 4–5 years

* is still very curious and asks lots of questions
* continues to enjoy imaginative and creative play activities
* continues to enjoy construction activities, spatial awareness increases
* knows, matches and names colours and shapes
* follows three-step instructions
* develops interest in reading for themselves
* enjoys jigsaw puzzles and games
* concentrates for longer (e.g. television programmes, longer stories) and can recall details
* shows awareness of right and wrong, the needs of others
* begins to see other people's points of view
* stores and recalls more complex information using language.

Age 5–8 years

* starts to learn to read
* enjoys some number work, but still needs real objects to help mathematical processes
* enjoys experimenting with materials and exploring the environment
* develops creative abilities as coordination improves (e.g. more detailed drawings)
* begins to know the difference between real and imaginary, but still enjoys imaginative play (e.g. small-scale toys, such as cars, play people, toy farm/wild animals)
* interested in more complex construction activities
* has longer attention span, does not like to be disturbed during play activities
* follows increasingly more complex instructions
* enjoys board games and other games with rules
* develops a competitive streak
* has increased awareness of right and wrong, the needs of others
* sees other people's points of view
* seeks information from various sources (e.g. encyclopaedia, Internet)
* processes expanding knowledge and information through language.

Baby playing with bricks

Ten ways to encourage a young child's intellectual development

1 Provide opportunities and materials to increase the child's curiosity (e.g. mobiles, posters, pictures, toys, games and books).

2 Encourage the child to be observant by pointing out details in the environment, such as: colours, shapes, smells, textures; interesting objects, such as birds, vehicles; talking about weather conditions; taking them on outings; gardening; keeping pets.

3 Participate in the child's play to extend learning by asking questions, providing answers and demonstrating possible ways to use equipment. Demonstrate how things work or fit together when the child is not sure what to do. For example, a child can become very frustrated when struggling to do a jigsaw, but make sure your help is wanted (and necessary) – use verbal prompts where possible to encourage children to solve the problem themselves.

4 Provide repetition by encouraging the child to play with toys and games more than once – each time they play, they will discover different things about these activities.

5 Provide gradually more challenging activities, but do not push the child too hard by providing activities which are obviously too complex – instead of extending the child's abilities this will only put them off due to the frustration at not being able to complete the task.

6 Remember safety. It is important to allow the child the freedom to explore their environment and to experiment with the properties of different materials. Make sure that these materials are suitable for a young child. Objects that can pose a choking hazard or glass objects that could be broken, causing cuts, must be kept well out of a baby's or young child's reach.

7 Encourage a child's auditory perception through activities such as singing rhymes and songs, clapping games, awareness of animal noises/environmental sounds, taped songs, rhymes, music, everyday sounds and stories, sharing books and stories, sound lotto, identifying musical instruments, speaking and listening activities.

8 Encourage a child's visual perception through activities involving exploration of the environment (e.g. outings to the park, farm), looking at books, pictures, displays, photographs, using magnification to highlight details (e.g. magnifying glass, binoculars, telescope), matching games, jigsaws, lotto, using mirrors, activities requiring letter and/or number recognition, including simple board games.

9 Encourage the child's tactile exploration through activities which involve exploratory play, such as handling sand, water, clay, dough, wood, using manufactured materials, such as plastic construction kits (LEGO®, Stickle Bricks®, Mega Bloks®), making collages using different textures, 'feely' box or bag.

10 Encourage use of taste and smell senses through cooking activities, finding out about different tastes (sweet, sour, bitter, salty) and different smells (sweet and savoury, flowers, fruit and vegetables). Remember safety.

EARLY LEARNING

Early learning involves learning through stimulating play activities with appropriate adult support to provide young children with the essential foundations for later learning. Young children who are pushed too hard by being forced to do formal learning activities before they are ready may actually be harmed in terms of their development and may also be put off reading, writing and other related activities.

The early learning goals for the Foundation Stage provide guidelines to help early years professionals (and parents) understand informal approaches to learning, including the importance of play in encouraging and extending all aspects of young children's development.

Early learning goals

✳ Personal, social and emotional development: encourages the development of young children's social skills, confidence and self-esteem; encourages young children to interact with other children through a wide range of play activities.

✳ Communication, language and literacy: help young children to develop their communication skills and early literacy skills by encouraging them to enjoy and participate in activities involving singing, talking and listening to stories;

parents and carers can also help by making time to read stories to young children and taking them to the local library.

❋ Mathematical development: helps young children develop early numeracy skills (e.g. counting, comparing, adding and subtracting); parents and carers can also help by playing number games and singing number rhymes/songs.

❋ Knowledge and understanding of the world: help young children to make sense of their environment (e.g. noticing changes in the seasons and weather).

❋ Physical development: encourages young children to be physically active by providing regular access to games, dancing/movement and outdoor play activities.

❋ Creative development: encourages young children to use their imagination and to express themselves creatively through activities such as dressing up, drawing, painting, model-making and music.

(QCA 2000)

(Further information about play and early learning is provided in chapter 10.)

DEVELOPING CHILDREN'S EARLY LITERACY SKILLS

Literacy involves the ability to read and write. Reading and writing are forms of communication based on spoken language. Young children need effective language and communication skills (see above) before they can develop literacy skills.

Learning to read and write

Learning to read involves the process of turning groups of written symbols into speech sounds. In English this means being able to read from left to right, from the top of the page to the bottom and being able to recognize letter symbols plus their combinations as words. Reading involves a variety of different skills, including visual discrimination, auditory discrimination, language and communication, word identification, conceptual understanding, comprehension skills, memory and concentration.

Being able to read does not happen suddenly. Reading is a complex process involving different skills. Being able to use and understand spoken language forms the basis for developing reading skills. A child who has a wide variety of language experiences will have developed many of the skills needed for learning to read.

Learning to write involves learning specific conventions with regard to letter shapes, the sequence of letters in words, word order in sentences, the direction of writing etc. It is usual to teach writing skills alongside reading. This helps young children to make the connection between written letters and the sounds they make when read. The activities used to develop children's reading skills will also help their writing skills. In addition, young children need plenty of opportunities to develop the coordination skills necessary for writing, such as hand-eye coordination, fine manipulative skills for pencil control and being able to sit still with the correct posture for writing.

Ten ways to help a young child develop early literacy skills

1 Provide opportunities for talking and listening: children who are effective communicators will transfer these skills to reading and writing.

2 Share books, stories, poems and rhymes (see below).

3 Play listening games (e.g. 'guess the sound', sound lotto and using everyday objects or musical instruments to encourage auditory discrimination).

4 Play matching games like snap, matching pairs and doing jigsaws to encourage visual discrimination.

5 Play memory games like 'I went shopping…' to develop concentration and memory.

6 Look at other printed materials (e.g. newspapers, magazines, comics and signs).

7 Have fun with letters (e.g. play 'I spy…' using letter sounds); go on a 'letter hunt' (look round the house for things beginning with a particular letter); hang up an 'alphabet washing line'; sing alphabet songs and rhymes.

8 Provide opportunities for the child to develop coordination skills, including drawing, painting, colouring in, tracing, threading beads, cutting and sticking and sewing (remember safety).

9 Provide opportunities for the child to form letters in a variety of ways: in the air, in sand, using paints, with crayons, pencils, felt tips, using plasticine or playdough.

10 Watch the television together: use appropriate children's programmes to encourage reading skills.

EXERCISE: How did you learn to read and write? Make a list of activities to help develop young children's reading and writing skills. You could include activities you have used or observed in nursery or school.

Sharing books and stories with young children

By sharing books with young children, you show them a positive attitude towards books and that reading is an important skill that is essential to everyday life. Sharing books and stories with young children is the most positive and interesting way to encourage them to want to read for themselves. The time spent sharing books and stories is also a special time, creating a positive bond between adult and child.

These times can have an almost magical quality for children, especially if the adult:

* develops interesting storytelling techniques, including visual aids such as puppets
* demonstrates clear and articulate 'reading aloud' skills (e.g. voice and tone changes)
* chooses appropriate and attractive books for the child
* has a wide repertoire of rhymes and songs to include in story sessions.

Encourage children (and their parents) to use their local library – remember, it's free! Check the family are aware of the library as a valuable local resource for all kinds of information (e.g. the Internet), not just books. Many libraries have story sessions for the under-fives; some even have special story/activity sessions and homework clubs (which help develop referencing skills) for children aged five-plus, as well as book-related activities during the school holidays.

Here are some general points to consider when choosing books and stories for children:

* attractive and colourful, with well-drawn, appropriate illustrations
* text appropriate for age and level of development (e.g. one/two sentences per picture, several sentences and some pages without pictures, text only books)
* safe for children and well made, in a variety of good quality materials
* images reflecting our multicultural society, the roles of men and women and people with special needs in positive ways
* homemade books about familiar objects and everyday life can be just as appealing as commercially produced books, especially to younger children
* photograph albums or books made using photographs of familiar objects, people and places
* books are a source of information, not just fun, so make sure the information provided represents the children's interests (include illustrated factual books, dictionaries, encyclopaedias and atlases)
* less is more! A small selection of quality books carefully chosen is better than a large collection of poor quality, unsuitable ones – remember to use the local library.

DEVELOPING CHILDREN'S EARLY NUMERACY SKILLS

Numeracy skills involve confidence and competence with numbers and measures, including understanding of the number system, knowing by heart various number facts (e.g. multiplication tables), making mental calculations, solving number problems in a variety of contexts, presenting information about counting and measuring, using graphs, diagrams, charts and tables.

Learning numeracy skills

Many children learn number names and how to count before they begin school. At home and/or in early years settings (e.g. day nursery or playgroup) they do counting activities and sing number songs and rhymes. From the age of about four to five years children begin to learn how to make mathematical calculations using real objects to add and subtract small whole numbers.

In addition to developing competency with numbers, children learn to recognize and name geometrical shapes. They also learn about the properties of shapes, e.g. a triangle has three sides; a square has four right angles. Children also learn about weighing and measuring, as well as learning to tell the time.

Five ways to help develop a young child's early numeracy skills

1 Provide sorting and counting activities, including stories, rhymes and songs (e.g. 'Goldilocks and the three bears'), matching games (e.g. lotto, snap), play activities, such as dressing up (e.g. pairs of socks, gloves, mittens) and organizing sets of plates, cutlery, boxes, toys in the home corner or play shop, using toy vehicles for counting and matching activities.

2 Provide games and activities to encourage understanding and use of numbers, including dominoes, snakes and ladders and other simple board games, looking for shapes/sizes and making comparisons, price tags and quantities in shop play and real shopping trips, number songs and rhymes (e.g. 'One, two, three, four, five/Once I caught a fish alive…').

3 Provide sequencing activities that involve comparing and ordering (e.g. in-set jigsaws, doll/toy sizes), putting events in order (e.g. stories, pattern of the day/week).

4 Provide weighing and measuring activities, such as shop play (using balance scales to compare toys and other items), real shopping (helping to weigh fruit and vegetables), sand play (heavy and light), cooking activities (weighing ingredients to show importance of standard measures). Encourage children to develop understanding of length by comparing everyday objects/toys and using mathematical language, such as tall/taller/tallest, short/shorter/shortest, long/longer/longest, same height, same length.

5 Provide opportunities for learning about volume and capacity using sand and water play, including filling various containers to encourage understanding of full, empty, half full, half empty, nearly full, nearly empty, more/less than, the same amount. Use coloured water to make activities more interesting. Gradually introduce idea of standard measures (e.g. litre of juice, pint of milk).

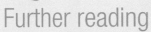

Further reading

Bruce, T. and Meggitt, C., 2002, *Child Care and Education*, 3rd edition, Hodder and Stoughton.

Hobart, C. and Frankel, J., 1999, *A Practical Guide to Activities for Young Children*, 2nd edition, Nelson Thornes.

Matterson, E., 1989, *Play with a Purpose for the Under-sevens*, 3rd edition, Penguin Books.

Matterson, E. (ed.), 1991, *This Little Puffin…Finger Plays and Nursery Games*, Puffin Books.

Meggit, C., 1999, *Caring for Babies: a practical guide*, Hodder and Stoughton.

Meggit, C. and Sunderland, G., 2000, *Child Development: an illustrated guide*, Heinemann Educational.

Petrie, P., 1989, *Communicating with Children and Adults: interpersonal skills for those working with babies and children*, Hodder Arnold.

Sheridan, M. *et al.*, 1997, *From Birth to Five Years: children's developmental progress*, Routledge.

Whitehead, M., 1996, *The Development of Language and Literacy*, Hodder and Stoughton.

Williams, S. and Goodman, S., 2000, *Helping Young Children with Maths*, Hodder and Stoughton.

Woolfson, R., 1999, *From Birth to Starting School: child development for nursery nurses*, *Nursery World* edition, Caring Books.

Children's emotions and behaviour 9

* Promoting young children's emotional wellbeing
* The expression of feelings
* Dealing with young children's fears and phobias
* Developing young children's social skills
* Promoting young children's positive behaviour
* Managing young children's behaviour
* Dealing with young children's difficult behaviour

PROMOTING YOUNG CHILDREN'S EMOTIONAL WELLBEING

Promoting young children's emotional wellbeing involves encouraging and supporting their emotional and social development.

You need to understand the sequence of young children's emotional and social development in order to provide them with appropriate assistance and support. Emotional and social development have been listed separately to assist your understanding of these two complex aspects of children's development, but you will notice that there are overlaps between the two aspects. The sequence of emotional development is outlined here; the sequence for social development is in the section on developing young children's social skills.

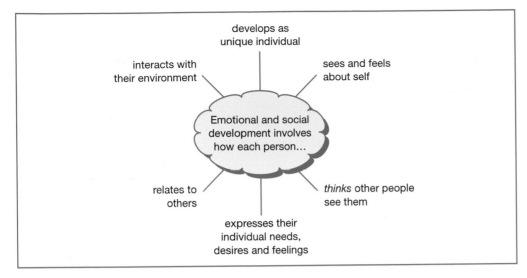

develops as
unique individual

interacts with
their environment

sees and feels
about self

Emotional and social
development involves
how each person…

relates to
others

thinks other people
see them

expresses their
individual needs,
desires and feelings

The sequence of emotional development: 0–8 years

Age 0–3 months

* becomes very attached to parent/carer (usually the mother)
* experiences extreme emotions (e.g. very scared, very happy or very angry); these moods change in an instant
* requires the security and reassurance of familiar routines
* may be upset by unfamiliar methods of handling and care.

Age 3–9 months

* has strong attachment to parent/carer (usually the mother)
* develops other attachments to people sees regularly
* by six or seven months shows clear preferences for familiar adults as can differentiate between individuals
* demonstrates strong emotions through body language, gestures and facial expressions
* dislikes anger in others and becomes distressed by it
* has clear likes and dislikes (e.g. will push away food, drink or toys does not want).

Age 9–18 months

* likes to get own way, gets very angry when adult says 'No!'
* has emotional outbursts (temper tantrums) when does not get own way or is otherwise frustrated (e.g. unable to do activity because of physical limitations)
* shows fear in new situations (e.g. attending parent/toddler group, visiting somewhere new such as the farm or nature centre)

* relies on parent/carer for reassurance and support in new situations
* is upset by the distress of other children (even if they caused it)
* seeks reassurance and contact with familiar adults throughout waking hours.

Age 18 months–2 years

* begins to disengage from secure attachment (e.g. wants to do things by self – 'Me do it!')
* still emotionally dependent on familiar adult(s), but this leads to conflict as need for independence grows
* has mood swings (e.g. clingy one moment, fiercely independent the next)
* becomes very frustrated when unable/not allowed to do a particular activity, which leads to frequent but short-lived emotional outbursts (temper tantrums)
* explores environment – even new situations are less frightening as long as parent/carer is present.

Age 2–3 years

* may still rely on parent/carer for reassurance in new situations or when with strangers
* still experiences emotional outbursts as independence grows and frustration at own limitations continues (e.g. aggressive towards toys that cannot get to work)
* begins to understand the feelings of others, but own feelings are still the most important
* has very limited understanding of other people's pain (e.g. if hits another child)
* feels curious about their environment, but has no sense of danger (e.g. that they or other people can be hurt by their actions).

Age 3–4 years

* less reliant on parent/carer for reassurance in new situations
* may be jealous of adult attention given to younger sibling or other children in a group
* argues with other children, but is quick to forgive and forget
* has limited awareness of the feelings and needs of others
* may be quite caring towards others who are distressed
* begins to use language to express feelings and wishes
* still has emotional outbursts, especially when tired, stressed or frustrated.

Age 4–5 years

* becomes more aware of the feelings and needs of others
* tries to comfort others who are upset, hurt or unwell
* may occasionally be aggressive as still learning to deal with negative emotions

- ✱ uses language to express feelings and wishes
- ✱ uses imaginative play to express worries and fears over past or future experiences (e.g. hospital visits, family disputes, domestic upheaval)
- ✱ has occasional emotional outbursts when tired, stressed or frustrated
- ✱ argues with other children, but may take longer to forgive and forget
- ✱ confidence in self can be shaken by 'failure'
- ✱ may have an 'imaginary friend'.

Age 5–8 years

- ✱ becomes less egocentric as understands feelings, needs and rights of others
- ✱ still wants things that belong solely to them (e.g. very possessive of own toys, puts own name on everything they possess!)
- ✱ becomes more aware of own achievements in relation to others, but this can lead to a sense of failure if feels does not measure up – hates to lose
- ✱ may be very competitive – rivalry may lead to aggressive behaviour
- ✱ argues with other children, but may take even longer to forgive and forget
- ✱ has increased awareness of the wider environment (e.g. the weather, plants and animals, people in other countries).

Young child engaged in imaginative play

Ten ways to promote a young child's emotional wellbeing

1 Be positive by using praise and encouragement to help the child focus on what they are good at. Point out all the things that make the child special.

2 Treat every child in the family as an individual. Each child has unique abilities and needs. Help them to maximize their individual potential.

3 Encourage the child to measure any achievements by comparing these to their own efforts. Foster cooperation rather than competition between children.

4 Have high but realistic expectations. Remember, 'nothing succeeds like success', so provide appropriate activities that are challenging but allow the child opportunities to succeed and enjoy learning in fun ways (see chapter 10).

5 Take an interest in the child's efforts as well as achievements. Remember that the way the child participates in activities is as important as the end results (e.g. sharing resources, helping others and contributing ideas).

6 Give the child opportunities to make decisions and choices. Letting young children participate in decision making, even in a small way, helps them to feel positive and important and also teaches them how to make appropriate judgements and sensible decisions later on.

7 Share books and stories about real-life situations showing children (and adults) that the child can identify with. Promote equality of opportunity by providing positive images of children and adults through books and stories as well as songs/rhymes.

8 Encourage the child to focus on their skills and abilities in positive ways (e.g. 'I can...' tree, with positive statements about what the child *can* do).

9 Provide opportunities for imaginative role-play that encourage the child to explore different roles in positive ways, e.g. dressing-up clothes, cooking utensils, dolls and puppets (see chapter 10).

10 Be consistent about rules and discipline. All children need consistency and a clearly structured framework for behaviour so they know what is expected of them (see later section in this chapter on managing young children's behaviour). Remember to label the behaviour, not the child, as this is less damaging to their emotional wellbeing (e.g. 'That was an unkind thing to say' rather than 'You are unkind').

THE EXPRESSION OF FEELINGS

Another essential aspect of promoting young children's emotional well-being is helping them to recognize and deal with their own feelings and those of other people.

Feelings can be defined as:

* an *awareness* of pleasure or pain
* physical and/or psychological *impressions*
* the *experience of emotions*, such as anger, joy, fear or sorrow.

There is an enormous range of emotions that are experienced by people as feelings. We all experience a variety of personal emotions that are related to our individual perceptions of self and our responses to life experiences. Personal emotions include:

* happiness, joy, pleasure, satisfaction
* sadness, grief, pain, despair
* enthusiasm, excitement, courage, impulsiveness
* reluctance, anxiety, caution, fear.

We also experience interpersonal emotions that affect the way we relate to other people and how they respond to us. Interpersonal emotions include:

* love, affection, kindness, acceptance
* hate, anger, malice, contempt
* respect, compassion, patience, trust
* jealousy, insensitivity, impatience, distrust.

Babies and very young children naturally demonstrate clearly how they feel by crying, shouting and rejecting objects. They will openly show affection and other emotions, such as jealousy or anger. Young children do not understand that others can be physically or emotionally hurt by what they say or do. Gradually, children become conditioned to accept that the feelings and needs of others *do* matter. Young children need to know that it is natural to feel a wide range of emotions and that it is acceptable to express strong feelings such as love and anger openly, as long as they do so in positive and appropriate ways.

You can help a young child to express their feelings through the following activities:

* books, stories and poems about feelings and common events experienced by other children to help the child recognize and deal with these in their own lives (e.g. *What makes me happy?* by Catherine and Laurence Anholt)
* creative activities to provide positive outlets for the child's feelings (e.g. pummelling clay to express anger, painting/drawing pictures or writing stories and poems which reflect their feelings about particular events and experiences)

* physical play or games involving vigorous physical activity that allow a positive outlet for the child's anger or frustration
* imaginative or role-play activities to act out the child's feelings (e.g. jealousy concerning siblings, worries over past experiences, fears about future events such as starting nursery or school, visits to the dentist or hospital).

Young children's emotional outbursts

Sometimes young children are overwhelmed by their emotions and will act inappropriately or regress to previous patterns of behaviour. Before young children are able to use language to express their feelings, they are more prone to demonstrate their emotional responses in physical ways (e.g. biting, scratching, kicking, shouting, screaming, throwing things, throwing themselves on the floor). These emotional outbursts or temper tantrums can be very frightening to the child and other children present. Adults, too, can find children's emotional outbursts difficult to deal with.

When dealing with a child's emotional outburst it is essential that you:

* remain calm yourself and speak quietly but confidently – shouting only makes things worse
* ignore the emotional outburst as far as possible while maintaining the child's safety
* avoid direct confrontations
* give the child time and space to calm down
* reassure the child afterwards but do not reward them
* when the child has calmed down, talk about what upset them in a quiet manner
* suggest to the child what they could do instead if they feel this way again.

The best way to deal with emotional outbursts is to minimize the likelihood of them happening in the first place. You can help minimize the likelihood of emotional outbursts by:

* avoiding setting up situations where emotional outbursts are likely to happen (e.g. avoid making unrealistic demands or doing complex activities when a child is tired)
* giving advance warning (e.g. preparing the child for new experiences or giving a five-minute warning that an activity is coming to an end and that you want them to do something else)
* providing reasonable choices and alternatives to give child a sense of responsibility and control (e.g. choice of next activity or choice of materials)
* making potential problem situations more fun and interesting to engage child's attention and cooperation (e.g. use toys to make bath-time or journeys more exciting)
* encouraging the child to express their feelings in more positive ways.

DEALING WITH YOUNG CHILDREN'S FEARS AND PHOBIAS

All young children feel frightened or worried sometimes. A fear is an emotion caused by a real or imagined danger – a feeling of anxiety caused by the anticipation of danger. A phobia is an irrational fear – a fear or hatred of a specific object, resulting in avoiding behaviour.

While phobias are extremely rare among young children, fears are a common aspect of their emotional development. Childhood fears can be very upsetting for the young child experiencing them and for the adult helping the child to cope with these fears.

Learning how to overcome fears helps to build the child's self-confidence. Most childhood fears are due to a child's:

❄ *reactions* from previous frightening experiences
❄ *expectations* concerning the unknown or new experiences
❄ *observations* of other people's responses to situations/experiences.

EXERCISE: Think about your own fears or phobias. For example:

❄ What were you frightened of as a child?
❄ Why were you frightened by it?
❄ How did you overcome this fear?
❄ Is there anything that frightens you as an adult?
❄ How do you cope with any fears or phobias now?

Being aware of your own fears and how you deal with them will increase your understanding of young children's fears and your ability to help them to cope. Most young children copy the reactions of other children or adults when responding to potentially frightening situations/experiences. Recognizing and coping with your own fears may stop you passing them on to children.

Common childhood fears	How you can help
Loud noises Many young children dislike loud, unexpected noises and can find storms with thunder and lightning particularly frightening.	Reassure the child by saying something like, 'I find thunderstorms noisy and scary too, but I tell myself it's only the clouds bumping into each other!' Tell the child they are safe.
Water Some children fear being sucked down the plughole while in the bath or being flushed down the toilet; they may be frightened by the noise or fear that a monster will come up and get them.	Tell them they are too big to go down the plughole or toilet. Do not pull the plug while the child is in the bath or flush the toilet while they are sitting on it. Use a child's seat on an adult toilet. Explain that there are no monsters in the toilet.
Monsters in the dark Being alone in the dark or seeing shadows may let the child's imagination run riot. They may dream of ghosts, monsters or other scary creatures.	Do not pass on own fears about the dark. Use a night-light or dimmer switch until child feels more confident. Tell them there are no monsters etc. Avoid scary stories or videos.
Insects and animals Some children fear crawling insects like spiders or buzzing insects like bees or wasps. Some children are scared of dogs or other animals.	Do not pass on own fears of insects or animals; many adults have a fear of spiders. Let trapped insects out the window or leave the room until the insect goes. Get the child used to seeing small animals in books, then in real life at a distance; when the child is confident, let them stroke a well-trained animal.

Ten ways to help a young child to cope with childhood fears

1 Acknowledge the child's fear by listening to them when they talk about it.

2 Do not pass on your own fears.

3 Do not rationalize irrational fears.

4 Remain calm and act confidently.

5 Reassure and comfort the child when they are frightened.

6 Let the child have comforters such as a favourite cuddly toy.

7 Let the child keep their distance from whatever frightens them; encourage them to get closer at their own pace.

8 Never force the child to face their fear before they are ready.

9 Prepare the child for potentially frightening experiences in advance (e.g. talk about it).

10 Read relevant stories to help alleviate fears (e.g. *Can't you sleep, little bear?* by Martin Waddell may help to dispel a young child's fear of the dark).

Remember, most childhood fears pass as quickly as they came and most fears disappear of their own accord, without any need for specialist help. Very rarely a fear becomes so severe that it dominates the child's life. A child's fear may be developing into a phobia if it:

✳ causes major disruption to the child's life
✳ necessitates rituals (e.g. checking under the bed several times)
✳ restricts behaviour so that the child avoids situations in case fear is present
✳ widens to include more fears (e.g. not just dogs but all animals)
✳ distorts the child's perceptions of reality.

Children with phobias need specialist help. Suggest to their parents that they discuss this with their GP, who may then refer the child to a child psychologist.

DEVELOPING YOUNG CHILDREN'S SOCIAL SKILLS

Developing young children's social skills is part of the socialization process. The socialization process involves the development of:

✳ acceptable behaviour patterns
✳ self-control and discipline
✳ independence, including self-help skills (e.g. feeding, toileting, dressing)
✳ awareness of self in relation to others
✳ positive relationships with others
✳ understanding the needs and rights of others
✳ moral concepts (e.g. understanding the difference between right and wrong, making decisions based on individual morality).

Young children model their attitudes and actions on the behaviour of others. They imitate the actions and speech of those they are closest to (e.g. acting out being 'mum', 'dad', 'nanny' or 'teacher', copying the actions and mannerisms of adults around the home or early years setting). All adults caring for young children need to be aware of the significant impact they make on children's emotional and social development by providing positive role models.

When caring for young children you should strike a balance between allowing for the child's increasing need for independence and providing supervision with appropriate guidelines for socially acceptable behaviour (see section on managing young children's behaviour).

The sequence of social development: 0–8 years

Age 0–3 months

❋ cries to communicate needs to others

❋ stops crying to listen to others

❋ responds to smiles from others

❋ responds positively to others (e.g. family members and even friendly strangers, unless very upset – when only main caregiver will do!)

❋ considers others only in relation to satisfying own needs for food, drink, warmth, sleep, comfort and reassurance.

Age 3–9 months

❋ responds positively to others, especially familiar people, such as family members (by nine months is very wary of strangers)

❋ communicates with others by making noises and participating in conversation-like exchanges

❋ responds to own name

❋ begins to see self as separate from others.

Age 9–18 months

❋ responds to simple instructions (if wants to!)

❋ communicates using (limited) range of recognizable words

❋ shows egocentric behaviour (e.g. expects to be considered first, all toys belong to them)

❋ is unintentionally aggressive to other children.

Age 18 months–2 years

❋ responds positively to others (e.g. plays alongside other children and enjoys games with known adults)

❋ communicates more effectively with others

❋ responds to simple instructions

❋ wants to help adults and enjoys imitating their activities

❋ may be interested in older children and their activities, imitates these activities

❋ may unintentionally disrupt the play of others (e.g. takes toys away to play with by self)

❋ becomes very independent (e.g. wants to do things by self)

❋ still demonstrates egocentric behaviour, wants their own way and says 'No!' a lot.

Age 2–3 years

❋ continues to enjoy the company of others

❋ wants to please and seeks approval from adults

* is still very egocentric and very protective of own possessions, unable to share with other children although may give toy to another child if adult requests it to please the adult
* may find group experiences difficult due to this egocentric behaviour
* uses language more effectively to communicate with others.

Age 3–4 years

* enjoys the company of others, learns to play *with* other children, not just alongside them
* uses language to communicate more and more effectively with others
* develops self-help skills (e.g. dressing self, going to the toilet) as becomes more competent and confident in own abilities
* still wants to please and seeks approval from adults
* observes closely how others behave and imitates them
* still fairly egocentric, may get angry with other children if they disrupt play activities or snatch play items required for own play and expects adults to take their side in any dispute
* gradually is able to share group possessions at playgroup or nursery.

Age 4–5 years

* continues to enjoy the company of other children, may have special friend(s)
* uses language even more effectively to communicate, share ideas and engage in more complex play activities
* appears confident and competent in own abilities
* cooperates with others, takes turns and begins to follow rules in games
* still seeks adult approval, will even blame others for own mistakes to escape disapproval
* continues to observe how others behave and will imitate them, has a particular role model
* may copy unwanted behaviour (e.g. swearing, biting or kicking) to gain adult attention.

Age 5–8 years

* continues to enjoy the company of other children, wants to belong to a group, may have a special friend
* uses language to communicate very effectively, but may use in negative ways (e.g. name-calling or telling tales) as well as positively to share ideas and participate in complex play activities, often based on television characters or computer games
* is able to play on own, appreciates own space away from others on occasions
* becomes less concerned with adult approval and more concerned with peer approval
* is able to participate in games with rules and other complex cooperative activities.

Young children engaged in dressing-up activity

Ten ways to help a young child develop social skills

1 Set goals and boundaries to encourage socially acceptable behaviour as appropriate to the child's age and level of development. Using star charts and other rewards can help.

2 Encourage the child to help tidy up. You could help the child design a certificate with a pledge such as, 'I promise to put away my toys every day'.

3 Encourage the child's self-help skills. Be patient and provide time for the child to do things independently (e.g. let young children dress themselves, as it is an essential self-help skill); remember that with practice they will get faster, so do not rush them.

4 Provide opportunities for play to encourage the child's self-help skills (e.g. dressing up helps young children learn to dress independently in a fun way).

5 Provide opportunities for the child to participate in social play (e.g. invite other children round to play, take the child to parent/toddler group, playgroup or nursery – see section on social play in chapter 10).

6 Use books and stories about everyday situations to help the child understand ideas about fairness, jealousy and growing up (e.g. Alfie books by Shirley Hughes).

7 Use puppets and play-people to act out potential conflict situations and help the child to work out possible solutions.

8 Encourage the child to take turns during play activities and games.

9 Encourage the child to share toys and other play equipment.

10 Encourage the child to focus on their own abilities. Emphasize cooperation and sharing rather than competition. Any comparisons should be related to the child improving own individual skills.

PROMOTING YOUNG CHILDREN'S POSITIVE BEHAVIOUR

Behaviour can be defined as a person's actions and reactions or a person's treatment of others. Behaviour involves young children *learning to conform* to adult expectations for behaviour. These expectations depend on the setting, the adult and their expectations of what is acceptable behaviour in relation to the child's age and level of development. What is acceptable in one situation may not be acceptable in another, even within the same setting (e.g. loud, boisterous behaviour *is* acceptable outside in the garden but *not* inside the house). Children who are not prepared (or are unable) to conform to these expectations have to accept the consequences, e.g. sanctions or punishments for unacceptable behaviour.

Ten ways to encourage a young child's positive behaviour

1 Keep rules to a minimum. Too many rules make it difficult for the child to remember and follow them. A child will often accept and keep to a few rules if they have some freedom. Children also need to learn self-control and make their own decisions regarding behaviour.

2 Be realistic about a child's behaviour. Accept that the child will be inquisitive, noisy and messy at times!

3 Be flexible. The child may behave inappropriately when own needs or wishes conflict with adult expectations. Changing some domestic routines to fit in with the child's individual needs may provide fewer opportunities for such conflicts. While clear structures and routines are essential, there should be room for flexibility, e.g. when the child is not responding well to an activity, be prepared to adapt or abandon the activity. Do less demanding activities when the child is tired, upset or unwell.

4 Be prepared to compromise. Negotiate goals and boundaries with the child. All children need to develop independence and have some control over their lives. Their wishes/ideas should be considered and respected. Give the child some freedom to:
    ※ explore and experiment (within safety limits)
    ※ select and carry out activities
    ※ choose and/or make snacks and meals
    ※ choose clothes and/or dress themselves.

Some activities and routines *have* to be done, but it may be possible to negotiate with the child as to *when* these tasks are done or give an incentive for completion (e.g. when they have finished tidying up, the child can choose a story or a rhyme).

5 Be positive. Once goals have been negotiated and set, encourage the child to keep them through rewards or other positive incentives. Reward positive behaviour using verbal praise, stickers or stars. Keep smiling! A sense of humour goes a long way.

6 Ignore certain behaviour. Ignore unwanted behaviour, especially attention-seeking or behaviour that is not dangerous or life-threatening (e.g. a toy left in the corner of a room will not hurt anyone, but left in the hallway or on the stairs could be a hazard).

7 Use diversionary tactics. Sometimes it is not possible or appropriate to ignore unwanted behaviour (e.g. if the child is in danger). With a younger child it may be more effective to distract the child (e.g. by playing a game) or to divert their attention to another activity (e.g. giving them another more suitable toy, while quietly taking the other one away). Diversionary tactics can often avoid the confrontations that can lead to emotional outbursts. Recognize and try to avoid the possible triggers to unwanted behaviour (e.g. avoid doing demanding tasks when the child is tired).

8 Be consistent. Once rules, goals and boundaries have been negotiated and set, stick to them. Children need to know where they stand and they feel very insecure if rules and boundaries keep changing for no apparent reason. The child needs to understand that 'no' always means 'no', especially where safety is concerned.

9 Give clear instructions and explanations. Explain why certain rules are necessary (e.g. for safety). Gradually the child will understand the need for rules and this will help them to develop their own self-control.

10 Keep calm. Be calm, quiet, firm and in control – shouting only makes matters worse. If you feel you are losing control, count to five and then proceed calmly. You may need to use strategies like time-out to give the child a chance to calm down, but keep it short (e.g. only a few seconds until the child is a little calmer).

MANAGING YOUNG CHILDREN'S BEHAVIOUR

Parents have social expectations relating to their children's behaviour based on cultural and religious beliefs, individual variations in childrearing practices or adherence to traditional childrearing practices. Traditionally, children did not dare challenge parental authority for fear of physical punishment. Today some parents still feel that if *they* were brought up this way, this is what they expect from their children. In the twenty-first century, society recognizes the rights of the child and has the expectation that all parents should be more caring and responsive to their children's needs by using positive methods such as praise, encouragement, negotiation and rewards to achieve socially acceptable behaviour. The UN Convention on the Rights of the Child states that 'children have the right to be protected from all forms of physical and mental violence and deliberate humiliation'.

Problems can arise if you and the child's parents have very different views on children's behaviour. Parents are often more lenient over their children's behaviour, especially if they feel guilty about being out at work all day. As a nanny you may have to deal with the resulting difficult behaviour demonstrated by a child spoiled by their parents' over-indulgence.

When agreeing standards of children's behaviour and discipline methods, you should remember to:

* keep an open mind about parental attitudes and expectations

* be prepared to compromise

* express your feelings or concerns tactfully

* be willing to exchange ideas

* be diplomatic when suggesting changes to the child's routine.

Sometimes parents will not see your point of view about managing young children's behaviour. As they are your employers, you must accept their way of dealing with their child's behaviour. You should be flexible and accept that there are limits to what you can achieve in terms of a child's behaviour and how much you can interfere. If you disagree strongly with the parents' childrearing practices (e.g. discipline methods that are too lenient or too strict), you should consider applying for another job.

After consultation with the child's parents, you will need to establish rules for behaviour as appropriate to the child's age and level of development.

Behaviour guidelines for babies

Babies have limited comprehension and communication skills, so negotiating goals and boundaries is not possible because they cannot understand what is required or be reasoned with. You can demonstrate what behaviour is required by providing a positive role model for behaviour. Babies are not deliberately naughty, so sanctions or punishments for unwanted behaviour are not appropriate. Babies may display difficult behaviour, such as persistent crying or being irritable or uncooperative, because these are the only ways they have to communicate things like hunger, tiredness, illness, anxiety or frustration.

You can establish the foundations of future rules for behaviour by:

* being calm – do not get annoyed with babies' behaviour

* praising and rewarding desired behaviour (ignoring unwanted behaviour)

* giving the baby appropriate care and adult assistance

* making potentially difficult situations more fun (e.g. using games and rhymes during routines such as mealtimes, nappy changing, dressing)

* being positive! (try not to say 'Don't...' or 'No' too often)
* using diversionary tactics (e.g. removing the baby from the situation or removing the object from the baby's reach)
* not forcing the baby to behave in certain ways (e.g. aggressive adult behaviour such as shouting only frightens babies and does not change their behaviour)
* NEVER using physical punishment (e.g. smacking, shaking) as this can cause serious or even fatal injuries to a baby (in any case, such punishment does not work as babies have no understanding of what they are being 'punished' for).

As babies develop, they become more independent; they will demonstrate this through challenging behaviour because they still lack the communication skills to express their needs effectively and are often frustrated by their lack of physical skills to do what they want. For example:

* challenging or refusing adult's choices of food, clothing and activities
* asserting own likes and dislikes
* starting to have frequent emotional outbursts or temper tantrums.

Behaviour guidelines for toddlers

Adults need to have realistic expectations for very young children and accept that certain types of behaviour are characteristic of the under-threes. For example, toddlers may be:

* attention-seeking – they dislike being ignored, so will interrupt adults
* very sensitive to changes and become upset if separated from parent or carer
* very active and keen to explore environment
* unaware of potential dangers
* unable to respect the possessions of others
* stubborn and insist on having their own way
* easily frustrated and prone to emotional outbursts
* unpredictable and contrary, with changeable behaviour.

The behaviour guidelines for babies also apply to toddlers, but in addition the under-threes need a positive framework for behaviour. You can encourage a toddler to behave in socially acceptable ways through:

* positive interaction with adults (and older children)
* opportunities for channelling their frustration through play
* diversions to distract the child from unwanted behaviour
* clear and consistent guidelines about what is and is not acceptable behaviour.

Behaviour guidelines for young children

When establishing rules for a young child's behaviour you will need to:

* see things from the child's point of view
* respect the child's ideas and needs
* teach the child to respect other people and their possessions
* help the child to develop self-control
* realize the child will test boundaries from time to time
* have realistic expectations for the child's behaviour
* recognize the limitations of a young child's level of understanding and memory skills.

Young children need to be active participants, not only in following rules, but also in establishing them. Young children are more likely to follow rules if they have some say about them. Having a feeling of ownership makes rules more real and gives young children a sense of control.

Rewards

Rewards can provide positive incentives for positive behaviour. Always use verbal praise and encouragement to reward the child's positive behaviour. Young children can also be motivated by rewards such as choice of favourite activity, smiley faces, stickers or badges, star charts, special certificates, special treats or outings.

Sanctions

You and the child's parents should agree on a scale of sanctions for inappropriate behaviour. Outline the sanctions to the child and explain why these sanctions are necessary. Effective sanctions should be designed to discourage inappropriate behaviour rather than to punish children who break the rules. Consistency in the application of sanctions is essential and adults should use reprimands sparingly and fairly. Sanctions are more likely to discourage inappropriate behaviour if young children see them as fair.

Sanctions for inappropriate behaviour may include:

* adult registering disapproval and explaining why to the child
* verbal warnings to the child that their behaviour is unacceptable
* 'time-out' involving isolation of the child for a very short period (see below)
* extra or alternative tasks for the child
* child losing a privilege (e.g. loss of special treat or outing).

Applying sanctions can be difficult, especially if your views on discouraging inappropriate behaviour differ from the parents. You should avoid telling the child off or imposing sanctions when the parent is at home and obviously in charge of the children. You should never interfere between the parent and child, especially if they are arguing.

Problems may arise over the use of physical punishment for inappropriate or unwanted behaviour. At the moment a nanny can smack a child with the parent's permission. However, as a childcare professional, you should not find it necessary to resort to physical punishment to control a child's behaviour. There are other more effective ways to deal with unacceptable or inappropriate behaviour (see above). Even if you do have the parent's permission to smack the child, I would not use this method of punishment as not only is it damaging to children (especially to their self-esteem), but it also leaves you open to possible allegations of child abuse if things go wrong.

Dealing with unacceptable behaviour using physical punishment is also inappropriate as it teaches young children that violence is an acceptable means of getting your own way. Smacking and shouting do not work; adults end up smacking harder and shouting louder to get the desired behaviour. Young children do not learn anything by being smacked; they are just hurt and humiliated.

DEALING WITH YOUNG CHILDREN'S DIFFICULT BEHAVIOUR

The adult response to a child's behaviour is as important as the behaviour itself. Different people have different attitudes as to what is or is not acceptable behaviour. The social context also affects adult attitudes towards children's behaviour (see above). All adults should consider certain types of behaviour unacceptable; these include behaviour that causes:

* physical harm to others
* self-harm
* emotional/psychological harm to others
* destruction to property.

Children are more likely to demonstrate difficult behaviour if they are:

* under-stimulated
* bored or frustrated
* uncertain of what is required (e.g. rules are unclear or unrealistic)
* with adults who have low/negative expectations for children's behaviour and learning.

Ten ways to respond to a young child's difficult behaviour

1 Be patient. Changing a child's behaviour takes time, so do not expect too much at once. Take things one step at a time. Remember that the child's behaviour may get worse before it gets better because the child may resist attempts to change their behaviour and may demonstrate even more difficult behaviour, especially if minor irritations are being ignored.

2 Be consistent. You need to be consistent when responding to a child with difficult behaviour or the child becomes confused. You need to discuss and agree on responses to the child's behaviour with the parents. You need to work with the child's parents to provide a consistent framework for behaviour.

3 Use diversionary tactics. You can sometimes divert the child from an emotional or aggressive outburst or self-damaging behaviour. This does not always work, but often does. Be aware of possible triggers to challenging behaviour and intervene or divert the child's attention *before* difficulties begin. Being offered alternative choices or being involved in decision making can also divert a young child.

4 Help the child find alternative ways to gain attention. Most children want adult attention; it is the way they behave to gain attention that may need changing. Instead of being disruptive, the child needs to be encouraged to use more acceptable ways to get adult attention by asking or showing the adult that they have something to share.

5 Look at the environment. Identify and, where possible, change aspects of the home environment and routines that may be contributing towards the child's difficult or challenging behaviour.

6 Label the behaviour, not the child. Make sure any response to difficult behaviour allows the child still to feel valued without any loss of self-esteem (e.g. 'I like you, Tom, but I don't like it when you…')

7 Be positive. Emphasize the positive and encourage the child to be positive too. Phrase rules in positive ways (e.g. 'do' rather than 'don't'). Think about which aspects of difficult behaviour must be stopped and which can simply be ignored so that the child is not being told 'No' or 'Don't…' all the time.

8 Use praise, encouragement and rewards. Set realistic and achievable goals and use child's interests to motivate them. Use regular positive feedback to encourage the child to behave in acceptable ways and raise their self-esteem. Praise the child's *efforts* as well as achievements. Use the types of rewards that matter to the child.

9 Avoid confrontation if at all possible. Use eye contact and the child's name to gain/hold their attention. Keep calm, sound confident and in control. If the child is too wound up to listen, give them a chance to calm down (e.g. time-out, which involves isolating the child for a very short period – the child must remain in sight of the adult).

10 Give individual attention and support. This encourages children to share their worries or concerns with a trusted adult. Giving the child special individual attention reinforces positive behaviour and decreases the need for them to gain adult attention through difficult behaviour. Time-in involves the child talking one-to-one with an adult about their day, including reviewing positive aspects of the day.

When dealing with a young child's difficult behaviour you should remember to:

* ❋ **p**raise and reward acceptable behaviour
* ❋ **r**educe the opportunities for difficult behaviour
* ❋ **a**void confrontations
* ❋ **i**gnore minor aspects of difficult behaviour
* ❋ **s**tructure appropriate sanctions
* ❋ **e**stablish clear rules, boundaries and routines.

EXERCISE: Describe how you have responded to a young child with difficult behaviour.

Further reading

Dowling, M., 2000, *Young Children's Personal, Social and Emotional Development*, Paul Chapman.

Hobart, C. and Frankel, J., 1999, *A Practical Guide to Activities for Young Children*, 2nd edition, Nelson Thornes.

Lindenfield, G., 1994, *Confident Children*, Thorsons.

Masheder, M., 1989, *Let's Play Together*, Green Print.

Matterson, E., 1989, *Play with a Purpose for the Under-sevens*, 3rd edition, Penguin Books.

Meggit, C., 1999, *Caring for Babies: a practical guide*, Hodder and Stoughton.

Mortimer, H., 2002, *Behavioural and Emotional Difficulties*, Scholastic.

Mukherji, P., 2001, *Understanding Children's Challenging Behaviour*, Nelson Thornes.

Roberts, R., 2002, *Self-esteem and Early Learning (0–8s)*, Paul Chapman.

Sheridan, M. *et al.*, 1997, *From Birth to Five Years: children's developmental progress*, Routledge.

Train, A., 1996, *ADHD: how to deal with very difficult children*, Souvenir Press.

Woolfson, R., 1999, *From Birth to Starting School: child development for nursery nurses*, *Nursery World* edition, Caring Books.

Time for play 10

- The importance of play
- The role of play in young children's development
- Types of play
- Children's social play
- Planning for play and early learning activities

THE IMPORTANCE OF PLAY

Young children learn through play. The term 'play' is often used to refer to activities that are considered to be unimportant and frivolous by many people (notably some teachers, parents and especially politicians!). It is up to early years workers to stress the importance of play to those who are sceptical about its benefits.

Play enables young children to:

* learn about and understand the physical world

* develop individual skills and personal resources

* communicate and cooperate with others

* develop empathy for others

* make sense of the world in relation to themselves

* do their own learning, in their own time and in their own way.

Play is not an extra – something to be done to keep children quiet and occupied while adults are busy or as a reward for when other (more important) tasks have been done. Play is an essential part of development and learning, especially for babies and young children.

THE ROLE OF PLAY IN YOUNG CHILDREN'S DEVELOPMENT

Young children need a combination of real and imaginary experiences to encourage language and learning. This is why play is an important aspect of young children's thinking and learning. Young children need to handle objects and materials to understand basic concepts (e.g. in mathematics, using objects for counting and addition, such as buttons, cones, plastic cubes). Once children have plenty of practical experiences they can cope more easily with abstract concepts, such as written sums or mental arithmetic. Young children use play opportunities to encourage and extend the problem-solving abilities that are essential to developing their intellectual processes.

Play activities help to develop young children's thinking and learning by providing opportunities for:

* well-motivated learning
* challenging and interesting learning experiences
* children to take responsibility for their own learning and to gain independence
* cooperative work between children
* developing problem-solving skills and improving concentration
* encouraging imagination and creativity.

Play activities provide informal opportunities for young children to develop ideas and understand concepts through active learning and communication. Language is a key component in children's thinking and learning. Play is an invaluable way to provide opportunities for language and to make learning more meaningful for young children. Play enables children to learn about concepts in a safe and non-threatening environment. (There is more information on activities to help the different aspects of young children's development in chapters 8 and 9.)

Seven ways to promote a young child's learning through play:

1   Plan play carefully and think about what the child will learn from the activities.

2   Provide challenging and interesting play opportunities appropriate to the child's age, needs, interests and abilities.

3   Provide varied resources and encourage the child to use them.

4   Participate in the child's play to stimulate language and extend learning.

5   Encourage the child's own imagination and creative ideas.

6   Encourage social interaction during play (e.g. the child may need coaxing to join in or guidance on taking turns and sharing).

7   Link play activities to real-life situations (e.g. link shop play with real shopping trips).

TYPES OF PLAY

There are three main types of play activity:

1. Physical play: play activities that help young children develop their physical skills.

2. Exploratory play: play activities that help young children to understand the world around them by exploring their environment and experimenting with materials.

3. Imaginative play: play activities that help young children to express feelings and develop social skills.

Physical play

Young children must have plenty of opportunities for physical play (e.g. play apparatus, outdoor play, ball games and swimming). By using their whole bodies, young children learn to control and manage them. The more practice the child gets to develop gross motor skills, the more agile, coordinated and safe they will be as they get older. Using lots of energy in physical play is also fun

Toddler playing on a slide

and relaxing. Young children also need opportunities to develop their fine motor skills and hand-eye coordination (e.g. playing with stacking toys and jigsaws).

Physical play helps young children to:

* develop body awareness and awareness of spatial relationships
* understand positional relationships, e.g. in and out, over and under
* develop gross motor skills
* develop fine motor skills
* improve hand-eye coordination and visual perception.

Activities to encourage young children's physical play:

1 Outdoor play opportunities should be provided for young children every day (e.g. playing in the garden, going for walks, going to the park or playing at the playground). As well as the benefits of fresh air, outdoor play offers young children more space to develop gross motor skills, such as running, hopping, jumping, skipping, throwing and catching a ball, playing football, doing somersaults and cartwheels.

2 Play apparatus can be used indoors or outdoors, depending on the size of the equipment and the space available. Larger play equipment that cannot be easily (or safely) accommodated in the house can be used in outdoor play (e.g. push-pull toys, ride-on toys, dolls' prams, wheelbarrows, lawnmowers, tricycles, bicycles and climbing apparatus). When using play equipment, whether in the house, garden or at the playground, you must ensure that it is safe for use as well as appropriate for the child's age and size. Always check play apparatus before use (see chapter 7).

3 Fitting and stacking toys helps children to explore properties of shapes as well as developing fine motor skills and hand-eye coordination. Posting boxes are also useful.

4 Jigsaw puzzles also help children with shape recognition as well as developing fine motor skills and hand-eye coordination. A child's first jigsaws will have whole figures that lift out by a knob. The child later tackles standard jigsaws with a few large pieces, increasing the number of pieces as the child grows and improves their physical skills.

5 Ball games provide young children with opportunities to develop ball skills, such as throwing a ball, kicking a ball and catching a ball. Younger children need large, lightweight balls to practise their throwing and catching skills. As children get older, smaller balls, beanbags and quoits can be used to develop their skills of throwing with more accuracy.

6 Swimming is an excellent all-round physical activity. Babies can be introduced to swimming from as young as four months old (once they have had their immunizations). Introducing babies and young children to swimming helps build confidence in the water so they will be ready to learn to swim by the age of four or five years.

Exploratory play

Exploratory play encourages and extends young children's discovery skills. Play is an important way to motivate children and to assist thinking and learning in a wide variety of settings. Young children learn from play situations that give them hands-on experience. Exploratory play encourages young children to use their senses to discover the properties of different materials in pleasurable and meaningful ways (e.g. playing with sand encourages young children to consider textures and the functions of sand, getting the right consistency of sand to build sandcastles – too wet or too dry and the sand will not stick together).

Exploratory play helps young children to:

* understand concepts such as shape and colour
* explore the properties of materials (e.g. textures)
* understand volume/capacity and physical forces through sand and water play
* develop problem-solving skills
* devise and use own creative ideas.

Young child engaged in exploratory play

Activities to encourage young children's exploratory play:

1 Painting with brushes, sponges, string; finger painting, bubble painting, 'butterfly' or 'blob' painting, marble painting, wax resist painting; printing (e.g. with leaves, potatoes, cotton reels) and pattern-making (e.g. with rollers, stamps).

2 Drawing using pencils, crayons, felt tips or chalks on a variety of materials, including different kinds of paper, card, fabric and wood. Include colouring activities linked to the child's interest by drawing your own colouring sheets, buying ready-made colouring books or using free printable colouring pages from the Internet.

3 Model-making using commercial construction kits (e.g. LEGO Explore®, Mega Bloks®, Stickle Bricks®), wooden blocks or clean and safe 'junk' materials to create their own designs.

4 Collage using glue and interesting materials to create pictures involving different textures, colours and shapes, and provide an enjoyable sensory experience too.

5 Clay, playdough and plasticine can be used creatively; they are tactile too.

6 Cooking provides a similar experience to working with playdough or clay except that the end product is (usually) edible. Remember to include 'no cook' activities, such as icing biscuits or making sandwiches or peppermint creams.

7 Making music can provide opportunities for young children to explore different sounds and to experiment freely with musical instruments. Provide a portable box with a range of percussion instruments, including drum, tambourine, castanets, wood blocks, shakers, bell stick, Indian bells, triangle, xylophone and chime bars.

8 Water play with plain, bubbly, coloured, warm or cold water helps young children learn about the properties of water (e.g. it pours, splashes, runs, soaks). Provide small containers to fill and empty, as well as a sieve and funnel. Include suitable bath toys to make bath-time more fun and also to encourage exploratory play.

9 Sand play provides opportunities for exploring the properties of sand (e.g. wet sand sticks together and can be moulded, while dry sand does not stick and can be poured). Use 'washed' or 'silver' sand (not builder's sand, which might contain cement). Provide small containers and buckets to fill and empty, as well as a sieve and funnel. A sandpit with a cat-proof lid is ideal for use in the garden.

EXERCISE: Give examples of exploratory play activities from your own experiences of working with young children.

Imaginative play

Imaginative play provides opportunities for young children to release emotional tension and frustration or express feelings such as anger or jealousy in positive ways. Imaginative play also encourages young children to look at and feel things from another person's viewpoint, as well as developing communication skills to interact more effectively with others. Imaginative play activities, such as role-play and dressing up, enable young children to overcome fears and worries about new experiences or people, to feel more important and powerful and to feel more secure by being able to regress temporarily to earlier levels of development.

Imaginative play activities help young children to:

* develop language and communication skills
* practise and rehearse real-life situations
* improve self-help skills, such as getting dressed
* express feelings in positive ways
* share ideas and cooperate with other children.

Activities to encourage young children's imaginative play:

1   Pretend/role-play includes 'domestic play' (e.g. playing/imitating mum or dad, pretending to be a baby while other children act as parents, imitating other role models, such as carers, teachers, characters from television, books) and 'shop play' (e.g. post office, hairdresser's, café, where other roles can be explored). Pretending to visit the dentist, clinic, optician or hospital or setting up a home corner, a health centre or hospital can also provide for this type of play.

2   Dressing-up activities (including pretending to be parents, carers, teachers, television superheroes, characters from games consoles, kings and queens) allow children to experiment with being powerful and in control. Pretending to be someone else can also help children to understand what it is like to be that person and encourages empathy and consideration for others.

3   Dolls and puppets can help young children to deal with feelings of jealousy over a new baby; puppets are a useful way of providing children with a 'voice' and may encourage shy or withdrawn children to express themselves more easily.

4   Miniature worlds include play with small-scale toys such as doll's houses, toy farms and toy zoos, as well as vehicle play where children can act out previous experiences or situations while sharing ideas and equipment with other children; this can also help them establish early friendships.

EXERCISE: List examples of imaginative play activities from your own experiences of working with young children.

CHILDREN'S SOCIAL PLAY

Children go through a recognized sequence of social play. Younger children tend to engage in more solitary or parallel play activities because they are more egocentric, while older children are capable of more cooperative play activities as they can take turns, share play equipment and follow rules more easily. There will be times when quite young children can be engaged happily in play activities with some interaction with other children (associative play), such as dressing up, home corner, doing jigsaws, simple construction or painting. There will be occasions when older children become engrossed in solitary or parallel play activities with no interaction with other children (e.g. doing detailed drawings and paintings, building intricate constructions that require complete concentration to the exclusion of everyone else).

The sequence of social play is as follows:

* solitary play: playing alone
* parallel play: playing alongside other children without interaction
* associative play: playing alongside other children with limited interaction
* cooperative play: playing together
* complex cooperative play: playing together including following agreed rules.

Example of social play

A young child's level of social interaction during play activities depends on:
* the individual child
* the child's previous experiences of play

* the play activity itself
* the social context (e.g. the setting and other people present).

Play helps develop young children's social and emotional skills by providing opportunities for:

* learning and developing new social skills
* practising and improving existing social skills
* experimenting with new situations (e.g. anticipating what they might do in new situations)
* preparing for new experiences
* acting out past experiences
* expressing emotions in positive ways.

PLANNING FOR PLAY AND EARLY LEARNING ACTIVITIES

After discussions with the parents, you will need to plan and implement play and early learning activities for the young child or children you work with. When planning play and early learning activities, your overall aims should be:

* to meet the child's individual developmental and learning needs
* to build on the child's existing knowledge and skills
* to help the child achieve their full learning potential.

The planning cycle

You should observe and assess the child's existing learning, development and/or behaviour. Use this information to plan appropriate early learning activities to encourage and extend the child's abilities in specific areas (e.g. outdoor play to develop gross motor skills or dressing up to develop self-help skills). You can write down your plans for play and early learning activities in a diary, daily log or activity file. Your plans can be as brief or as detailed as you wish. Some activities may require more detailed preparation and organization than others.

A plan for an early learning activity could include the following:

Title   A brief description of the activity
When?   Date and time of the activity
Where? Where the activity will take place (e.g. lounge, kitchen, garden or park)
Why?   Why you have selected this particular activity (e.g. identified child's particular need through observation, links to topics or child's interests) and the main purpose of the activity (e.g. how it will encourage the child's development and learning – you could indicate what the child will gain from participating in the activity in each developmental area: social, physical, intellectual, communication, emotional)

| What? | What you need to prepare in advance (e.g. selecting or making appropriate materials, buying ingredients, materials or equipment) – think about any instructions and/or questions for the child |
| How? | How you will organize the activity, considering any safety requirements and thinking about tidying up after the activity (e.g. encouraging the child to help tidy up) |

Evaluate the activity afterwards (e.g. the child's response to the activity, the skills and/or learning demonstrated by the child, the success of the activity, the effectiveness of your preparation, organization and implementation). Make a note of your evaluation in the diary, daily log or activity file. These notes will prove helpful when you give the parents progress reports on the child's learning and development at regular meetings (see chapter 6).

Be flexible in planning activities

Careful planning of appropriate play and early learning activities for young children is necessary to ensure they have opportunities to develop knowledge and skills within a meaningful context. However, your planning should be flexible enough to allow for each child's individual interests and unplanned, spontaneous opportunities for language and learning (e.g. an unexpected snowfall can provide a wonderful opportunity to explore and talk about snow, as well as enabling the child to express delight and fascination for this type of weather).

Toddler playing on a snowy day

As well as activities you have planned, you should give young children the freedom to do self-chosen activities (e.g. using computers, drawing, painting, construction, pretend/role-play, sand or water play). It is important that young children have this freedom of choice to help represent their experiences, feelings and ideas. You will still need to supervise these activities and may still be involved in them, but in more subtle ways, such as encouraging the children to make their own decisions or talking with them while they do these types of activities.

EXERCISE: Think about how you plan play and early learning activities. Describe how you have used an unplanned learning opportunity.

Further reading

Bilton, H., 2004, *Playing Outside: activities, ideas, and inspiration for the early years*, David Fulton Publishers.

Broadhead, P., 2003, *Early Years Play and Learning: developing social skills and co-operation*, Routledge Falmer.

Bruce, T., 2001, *Learning Through Play: Babies, Toddlers and the Foundation Years*, Hodder and Stoughton.

Einon, D., 1986, *Creative Play*, Penguin.

Gibson, R., 1998, *Usborne Playtime Activities*, Usborne Publishing Ltd.

Hobart, C. and Frankel, J., 1999, *A Practical Guide to Activities for Young Children*, 2nd edition, Nelson Thornes.

Lindon, J., 2001, *Understanding Children's Play*, Nelson Thornes.

Masheder, M., 1989, *Let's Play Together*, Green Print.

Matterson, E., 1989, *Play with a Purpose for the Under-sevens*, 3rd edition, Penguin.

Meredith, S., 1988, *Teach Your Child To Swim*, Usborne Publishing Ltd.

Morris, J. and Mort, J., 1991, *Bright Ideas for the Early Years: learning through play*, Scholastic.

❋ Maintaining a healthy lifestyle

❋ How to make the most of your free time

❋ Developing your own social skills and social connections

❋ Nanny networks

❋ Socializing with the children

❋ Socializing with the family

❋ Outings

❋ Holidays and travel

MAINTAINING A HEALTHY LIFESTYLE

Working with young children is a rewarding but often challenging or even stressful occupation. You need to take responsibility for your own emotional well-being and take the necessary action to tackle or reduce stress in your life. To get the most out of your personal and professional life, you need to:

❋ develop and maintain confidence in your own abilities

❋ take care of your emotional wellbeing

❋ take regular exercise

❋ have a healthy diet

❋ make the most of your free time

❋ make new friends and develop new skills

❋ take time to relax and enjoy yourself!

HOW TO MAKE THE MOST OF YOUR FREE TIME

When working as a nanny (especially if you live in) it may be difficult to define clearly your working hours and free time. Most nannies have two days off per week, which are usually taken at weekends. You will also have most evenings free, but remember, normally you will be expected to do one to two evenings' babysitting per week.

Under the 1998 Working Time Regulations, nannies are entitled to a minimum of four weeks' paid holiday per year, to be taken at times as agreed with the family. You will usually be expected to take your own holidays when the family have theirs, but occasionally the family may wish you to go on holiday with them to help with the children (see below). You should normally have time off on bank holidays, but if this is not convenient for the family you may expect to receive extra payment and/or time off in lieu.

It is important to make the most of your free time, especially if you are a live-in nanny; you should not be stuck in your room every evening and weekend. You should try to get out of the house a few nights a week to meet other people, even if you are a daily nanny. While you may enjoy the independence of working as a nanny, you may feel lonely and isolated at times. Working with young children is a very demanding job and you need to spend your free time relaxing and enjoying the company of adults. Not only will this help to recharge your batteries, but it can also provide you with stimulating interests that will help your personal and professional development.

There are lots of ways that you can make the most of your free time. For example, you could improve your education and qualifications. Your employer may even offer to pay for you to attend work-related courses (e.g. paediatric first aid, managing children's behaviour). You may decide to have a go at doing something related to a particular hobby or interest that will also help you to develop new skills or make new friends. If you already have a circle of friends, you may enjoy going out with them in your free time or going on holidays with them.

You may want to visit a local snooker club, leisure centre, sports club, arts centre, concert venue, theatre or cinema, as well as pubs, nightclubs and other places people go to enjoy themselves. Try to make the most of your free time by becoming involved in whatever opportunities are available in your local area.

You can find out about what is available in your local area through:

* friends and family
* your employer (especially if you are new to the area)
* local newspapers and local radio
* libraries and information centres
* leisure centres
* theatres or cinemas
* voluntary organizations
* local colleges.

DEVELOPING YOUR OWN SOCIAL SKILLS AND SOCIAL CONNECTIONS

Feeling homesick

If you have relocated with the family to a new area or have relocated to start a new nanny job you may be feeling homesick. Everyone feels a little homesick when they first move to a new area. Relocating for a nanny job may mean living away from your family home for the first time, which can be a daunting experience in itself. When you move to a new area you will probably be worried about things like:

* What will the new area be like?
* How will I find my way around?
* How will I help the children to make new friends?
* How will I make new friends?

If you have relocated for a new nanny job you may have additional worries, such as:

* What will the children be like?
* How will I fit in with the family?
* Can I cope with the workload? (See chapter 5.)

Do not bottle up your worries or feelings of homesickness. Talk to someone such as your family and friends or even your employer. Being away from home, especially for the first time, can make you feel lonely and lost. Talking about it usually puts everything back into perspective. Remember to keep in touch with your family and friends by telephone, letters or email.

Making friends

Finding friends can be very hard work, especially if you have moved to a new area to take up a nanny position. Remember it is up to you if you want to make friends or not. We are all different. Some people are just happy to stay at home and curl up with a good book or watch a favourite television programme. If you are happy with very few or no friends, because you enjoy being alone and doing your own thing, that is fine. However, if you are alone because you are afraid of being with others or do not know how to find friends, you need to do something about developing your social skills and social connections.

If you want to make friends it is a good idea to look for people who enjoy doing the same sort of things you do or go to the same places you like to go to. The local college is a good place to start. Going to leisure centres, pubs and clubs are other ways to meet up with friends (see above).

Making friends is like anything else in life. For anything worthwhile you have to make an effort and work at it. When you meet new people, smile and be confident. Remember to be yourself. Real friends will want to know you for who you are, warts and all! To have a friend you need to be a friend. Being a friend means helping your friends and treating them as you would wish to be treated.

NANNY NETWORKS

If you are feeling very isolated, with little social life and no interaction with your peers, you could try to meet other nannies, for example, through a nanny support group. Find out if there is a nanny support group in your area. If not, consider asking your employer to help you start a nanny group. Your employer may be able to help by allowing the group to meet in the family home, providing the refreshments occasionally or, if they have the necessary expertise, offering to speak to the group about a relevant topic. A nanny group may also take the children on outings, have teddy bears' picnics, hold festive holiday parties, do art and craft activities together etc. The nannies in the group may also meet socially at weekends, without the children.

Joining (or setting up) a nanny group will provide you with opportunities to:

❋ make new friends
❋ discuss your views about working as a nanny
❋ share ideas about childcare and early learning activities
❋ improve your skills as a nanny.

You can use the Internet to find out about nanny groups as well as other ways to meet other nannies. For example, there are many 'nannies only' message boards on nanny or childcare websites where you can communicate with other nannies via email about professional matters or just have a chat. Some websites have established a database to enable you to find and link up with other nannies in your area. Some websites have a directory of new and existing nanny circles that can be accessed by members only. (See Appendix: Useful information for how you can find a nanny support group or other places to meet other nannies.)

EXERCISE: Find out about nanny support groups and other places to meet nannies in your area.

SOCIALIZING WITH THE CHILDREN

Meeting other nannies (and their charges) is not only good for your personal and professional development, but is also beneficial for the child or children you look after, as they get additional opportunities for social interaction with other children.

You should also be involved in providing opportunities for the children to meet and play with their friends, such as:

❋ taking the children to clubs and/or activities (e.g. swimming lessons, gym classes, Rainbow Guides, Beaver Scouts)

❋ inviting other children/friends to the family home

❋ visiting other children/friends in their homes

❋ organizing birthday parties for the children

❋ taking the children to birthday parties and other celebrations.

You will also be responsible for taking the children to groups where they can socialize with other children of a similar age, such as parent/carer and toddler group, playgroup or nursery.

SOCIALIZING WITH THE FAMILY

As already mentioned, you will be socializing with the family to some degree, for example, mealtimes, birthdays and other special occasions, especially if you are a live-in nanny. While you may be involved in some aspects of the family's social life, such as birthdays and holidays, to be an effective nanny you should always keep a certain level of professional detachment. Close personal friendships with the parents or other family members should be avoided as they can complicate your working relationship with the parents and confuse the child. In addition, if you fall out socially this will make it virtually impossible for you to continue working for your employer (see chapter 6).

OUTINGS

Outings provide excellent opportunities for you to encourage and extend all aspects of young children's development and learning. There are many different places where you can take young children on outings. Some outings are short, simple, cheap and easy to organize. Other outings take more organization, involve a whole day and can be more exciting, but also more expensive. Outings can be divided into indoor and outdoor activities:

Examples of indoor activities include:

❋ art gallery

❋ aquarium

❋ butterfly centre

* cinema
* gym tots
* indoor adventure play/soft play centre
* library
* museum
* swimming pool
* theatre
* toy library.

Examples of outdoor activities include:

* airport viewing gallery to watch planes
* bird sanctuary
* botanical gardens
* bug hunt
* castle
* farm
* nature walk
* park and pond with ducks to feed
* safari park or zoo
* seaside
* train station to watch trains, especially steam engines
* wildlife park.

Young child visiting a farm in spring

The types of outings you organize will depend on the child's interests, age and level of development, as well as what is available to do in your area. You can find out about activities and places of interest for young children at your local library or information centre.

Ten golden rules for outings with young children

All outings with young children should be both safe and enjoyable. To make this possible, follow these ten golden rules:

1 Check the outing is suitable for the age and level of development of the child.
2 Obtain permission from the child's parents.
3 Ensure the destination, leaving time and expected return times are in the daily log.
4 Know how to get there, e.g. location, route and mode of transport.
5 Check the seasonal conditions, weather and time available.
6 Assess any potential dangers or risks, e.g. activities near water, suitability and safety of playground equipment.
7 Ensure the child's safety at all times, e.g. never leave unattended, use five-point harness when using pram/pushchair or walking with toddlers.
8 Carry essential information/equipment such as identification, emergency contact numbers, mobile phone, first aid, spare clothing, food, money and any medication.

Toddler on an outing to the seaside in winter

9 Make sure you and the child are suitably dressed for the occasion, e.g. sensible shoes or boots for walks, waterproof clothing for wet weather, sunhat and sunscreen in hot weather, clean, tidy clothes for cinema, theatre, museum visits.

10 Talk to the child about their surroundings during the outing and take it slowly by proceeding at the child's pace.

EXERCISE: Find out about activities and places of interest for young children's outings at your local library or information centre.

HOLIDAYS AND TRAVEL

Holidays with the family

When taking holidays with the family, you can expect to work your usual hours and be paid your regular salary. However, it is not unusual to be expected to work longer hours, for example, babysitting most evenings so the parents can go out by themselves. If this is the case, you should be paid your usual overtime rate for any extra hours. Your employer should pay for your airfare, meals, accommodation and any other travel-related expenses. Your employer should also pay for your admission to theme parks, shows and other attractions when you accompany them and the child or children. You may also be given a larger kitty than usual for reasonable expenses when caring for the child on holiday, so that you can take them out and about. Remember that while this is not *your* holiday, when you do have some time off you will have to pay for your own entertainment and eating out, just as you would on your days off at home.

It is important to plan, discuss and document what your exact working arrangements will be *before* you go on holiday with the family. If possible have a look on the Internet for ideas about the types of activities available for young children at the holiday destination, as well as what is available for you to do and enjoy on your days/times off. Make sure you plan how you will look after the child on holiday. Remember that the child's routine may be very different while on holiday, for example, some children do not sleep or eat well when away from home. Most young children, especially toddlers, are more difficult to look after in a strange environment, because they do not like change and miss their familiar surroundings, toys and friends. You should stick to the child's usual routine as far as is practical (e.g. mealtimes, nap-times and bedtimes) and keep the child occupied with enjoyable activities.

Travelling with young children

When travelling on holiday with young children, it is helpful for you to talk with the parents and plan everything for the children well in advance.

12 ways to ensure safe and enjoyable holidays with young children

1   Suggest a child-friendly holiday (e.g. seaside with quiet family beach, family campsite or similar child-friendly destination). Avoid crowded, over-stimulating tourist attractions and city breaks.

2   Help the child prepare for the holiday by looking at pictures of the holiday destination in the brochure and talk about the sorts of activities you will be doing there.

3   Be positive about the holiday so the child can pick up your positive feelings and look forward to it with excitement.

4   If you and the family are travelling by car, make sure the child's car seat is properly installed (see chapter 7). Use removable window shades to keep the sun off the child.

5   When travelling, keep handy a change of clothes, a small first aid kit (including any medicines and creams usually required for the child) and carrier bags (for rubbish and sickness).

6   While on holiday always remember the child's sunhat and sunscreen (factor 30). Babies aged six months or less should be kept out of the sun, while older babies and young children should have very limited exposure, especially between 11 a.m. and 3 p.m. on hot and sunny days.

7   Always remember the child's safety. Pack a simple childproofing kit to use at your holiday destination. Remember to follow the golden rules for outings (see above).

8   Take bottled water and some healthy snacks for the journey. Young children can get dehydrated quite quickly, especially during a long flight or car journey. Make sure you have baby wipes for cleaning up after snacks.

9   When travelling by car, have frequent breaks to give the child the chance to stretch their legs and run around. Set off early in the day so that everyone has a chance to relax and unwind when you get to the holiday destination.

10 Keep the child occupied. Pack a goody bag to help keep the child entertained during the journey. Include favourite toys, games, books and some surprises appropriate to the child's age, e.g. rattles, musical toys, soft animals, pop-up toys or plastic keys for babies; puzzles, puppets, songs/rhymes on cassettes, story cassettes and picture books for young children. Play games like 'I spy...', using colours or letter sounds.

11 Be flexible – travelling on holiday with young children can be an enjoyable experience as long as you go with the flow. Try not to over-stimulate young children with too many new experiences or activities. Keep your holiday itinerary simple (e.g. plan only one major activity a day). Adjust your plans if the child gets tired or bored.

12 Use a disposable camera so the child can record holiday moments. When you return home, help the child to compile a scrapbook about the holiday, including photographs, postcards, drawings and other small souvenirs.

Further reading

Bradley, C. and Fitzsimons, C., 1999, *Outdoor Activities for Kids: over 100 fun, practical things to do outside*, Lorenz Books.

Clarke, J., 2004, *Body Foods for Busy People*, Quadrille Publishing Ltd.

Goleman, D., 1996, *Emotional Intelligence*, Bloomsbury.

Gore-Lyons, S., 2003, *Travelling Abroad with Children*, Arrow.

Lindenfield, G., 2000, *Self-esteem: simple steps to developing self-reliance and perseverance*, HarperCollins.

Matthews, A., 1990, *Making Friends: a guide to getting along with people*, Media Masters.

Murphy, S., 2004, *My Fitness Journal*, Ryland, Peters & Small.

Roet, B., 1998, *The Confidence To Be Yourself*, Piatkus.

Tucker, S., 2002, *Have Toddler Will Travel*, Hodder Mobius.

❀ Leaving a nanny position

❀ Submitting your resignation

❀ Getting the sack

❀ Leaving the children

❀ Keeping in touch with the family

❀ Moving on to another job working with children

❀ Working abroad with children

LEAVING A NANNY POSITION

You may be leaving a nanny position for a variety of reasons, such as:

❉ your contract is coming to an end (e.g. temporary nanny job)

❉ changes to the family's childcare needs (e.g. all the children will be at school full time)

❉ you have problems with the family that cannot be resolved

❉ the family is relocating and you are not going with them

❉ you wish to move to another nanny job or change career

❉ you decide to go into full-time further or higher education.

When leaving a nanny position you should give the family as much notice as possible. It is usual to give your employer one month's notice of your intention to leave or whatever timescale is stated in your contract. Remember you are a childcare professional and should give the children time to adjust to the fact that you are leaving. You also need to give the parents time to make appropriate alternative childcare arrangements.

You should never leave a job without giving notice, for example, in the heat of the moment following a dispute with the family. Not only is it unprofessional, it is also detrimental to the emotional well-being of the children. The children need the chance to say goodbye to you (see below).

SUBMITTING YOUR RESIGNATION

As a courtesy you should tell your employer face-to-face of your intention to leave, as well as giving them notice in writing. Here is an example of a letter of resignation:

---

21 June 2004

Dear Mr and Mrs Jones,

It is with some regret that I tender my resignation. I am giving you one month's notice (as required in my contract of employment dated 10 January 2002) of my intention to leave my position of nanny to your son, Tom.
I have enjoyed looking after Tom and am sure that we have both gained from the experience.
Thank you for being such friendly and considerate employers. I especially wish to thank you for your encouragement and support regarding my continued childcare studies.
Wishing you and Tom all the best for the future,

Yours sincerely,

GETTING THE SACK

Getting the sack is probably one of the worst experiences for a nanny. Your employers should give you an explanation for their decision to terminate your employment. For example:

* the children have started full-time school and the family no longer require a nanny
* one of the parents has lost their job
* the family is relocating
* you have behaved unprofessionally (e.g. always late or not turning up for work)
* you and the family are incompatible or have difficulties that cannot be resolved.

Whatever the reason, getting the sack can be an uncomfortable experience for both you and the family. You should continue to work for the family during your notice period but, depending on the reasons for your termination, it can be difficult working for someone who obviously does not want you there. Your employers may decide that it is best for all concerned that you leave immediately and they pay you in lieu of notice, especially if they have any concerns about the welfare of their children.

Your employer should terminate your employment in person as well as in writing. You and the family should be clear about what was agreed with regard to terminating your employment as stated in your contract of employment, e.g. one month's notice in writing, grounds for instant dismissal (see chapter 4). As well as informing you of the reasons for terminating your employment, your employer should also let you know whether you can expect a favourable reference from the family or if they would prefer that you did not use their name as a reference. Your final salary payment, any holiday pay and/or any pay in lieu of notice should be paid immediately by your employers on your leaving date.

If you are having to leave through no fault of your own (e.g. the family no longer require a nanny because their childcare needs have changed), you can ask your employer to write you a favourable letter of recommendation and/or act as a referee to assist you in your search for future employment.

LEAVING THE CHILDREN

If your job as a nanny has been a successful one and you are leaving under amicable circumstances, it can be quite upsetting when the time comes for you to leave, especially for the children. The children may react to the news that you are leaving in a variety of ways, e.g. showing no visible concern, being more clingy than usual or demonstrating difficult behaviour. You should respond to the children's reactions with patience and reassurance.

Talk to the children about what you will be doing next, e.g. going to college, working abroad, returning to your family, getting married. Reassure the children that you will still be thinking of them and continue to care about them, even though you are no longer their nanny. If you do not have any photographs of you and the children, arrange with the parents to have some taken so that the children can put them in their scrapbooks and you can have a reminder of them as well. If you are introduced to the new nanny and asked to stay on during their first week, you should help them to become familiar with the family home as this will enable a smoother transition for the children (see chapter 5).

Nanny and children

KEEPING IN TOUCH WITH THE FAMILY

With the parents' permission, tell the children that you will keep in touch by telephone, letters/postcards or even the occasional visit. Keep the family informed about what you are doing and ask them about the children's progress, especially at Christmas and the children's birthdays. (I am still in contact with families for whom I worked as a nanny and the children are now at university!) In some circumstances, such as leaving the job to study full time, it may be appropriate for you to continue seeing the children on a regular basis, e.g. babysitting one evening per week and/or looking after the children during the new nanny's holidays. However, depending on the reasons for termination, your employers may prefer not to be contacted in the future or that you to do not keep in touch with the children.

MOVING ON TO ANOTHER JOB WORKING WITH CHILDREN

There are various job opportunities available for childcare professionals who wish to work with children, including:

* au pair (see later section in this chapter on working abroad)
* childminder
* children's holiday representative (see section on working abroad)
* children's nurse
* maternity nurse (see chapter 1)
* nursery nurse/nursery assistant
* playworker
* social worker
* special needs nanny (see chapter 1)
* teacher
* teaching assistant.

Childminder

A childminder is self-employed and looks after children in the childminder's own home. To look after children under the age of eight, a childminder must be registered with and be inspected by the Office for Standards in Education (Ofsted). The exact terms and conditions of employment are negotiated between the childminder and the children's parents. A childminder should provide physical care and intellectual stimulation, including play opportunities, to assist the children's development and learning. They may also take children to and from playgroup, nursery class or school. Most childminders have children of their own. Contact your local social services department or your local council's childcare information service (if they have one) to find out about becoming a childminder in your area. For further information contact the National Childminding Association: www.ncma.org.uk.

Children's nurse

A children's nurse cares for sick children and provides support to their families. Normal entry requirements are a minimum age of $17^1/_2$ years and five GCSE passes or equivalent at grade C or above in English Language or Literature and a science subject. The NHS welcomes people with alternative academic and vocational qualifications, for example, the CACHE Level 3 Diploma in Child Care and Education or the Edexcel Level 3 BTEC National Certificate or Diploma in Early Years. For more information contact the Nursing and Midwifery Admissions Service: www.nmas.ac.uk.

Nursery nurse/nursery assistant

A nursery nurse provides care and education for children from birth to eight years. She/he plans and supervises play and early learning activities to help young children's development and learning, and may work in a nursery school, primary school, special school, day nursery or hospital. Day nurseries may be run by a voluntary or community group, local authority, private company or employer with a nursery for the children of staff members. Day nurseries usually provide full day care and education for young children up to the age of five years, with usual opening hours of 8 a.m. to 6 p.m. Monday to Friday. In a managerial role (e.g. nursery manager or nursery officer), as well as planning and supervising activities for the children, you would also be responsible for supervising staff and business administration. Nursery assistant jobs are for people with Level 2 childcare and education qualifications and for childcare professionals working under supervision. For more information contact your local council, local education department or the National Day Nurseries Association: www.ndna.org.uk.

Playworker

A playworker is responsible for the care and education of children aged 4–14 years in a variety of settings, including breakfast clubs, after-school clubs and holiday play schemes. Hours vary according to the type of setting. Job opportunities for playwork are available through voluntary organizations, local authorities or charities, in schools, community centres and leisure centres. There is a wide range of activities on offer to children, including play (both indoors and outdoors), sports, drama, music, arts and crafts, as well as help with homework. For more information contact the National Network of Playwork Education and Training: www.playwork.org.uk.

Social worker

To work as a social worker requires a professional qualification. There are various ways to enter the social work profession, depending on your age and previous experience. Many people enter social work as a second or third career. Your previous experience may be taken into account, as well as any formal academic qualifications, when considering your eligibility to join a degree course. The degree can be studied through full-time, part-time and distance-learning programmes. Where appropriate, previous academic experience may be taken into account and some form of credit given. Most social workers work with a range of different client groups during their working life. After graduation you can choose to specialize in work with children and families. For further information see the Social Work Recruitment Campaign website: www.socialworkcareers.co.uk.

Teacher

Teaching in a primary school involves working with children aged 3–11 years. Teaching is an excellent opportunity for working with children and can be an ideal career for those who enjoy working with children. A teacher in a primary school teaches all subjects of the National Curriculum. There are two main routes into teacher training:

1   Studying for a first degree that includes a teaching qualification, e.g. Bachelor of Education degree. Applicants normally need at least two A levels and three GCSEs (grade C or above) in other subjects.

2   Studying for a first degree, then taking a one-year full-time teacher training course, e.g. Post Graduate Certificate in Education (PGCE).

You may also be able to gain entry to a teacher training course with one of the following:

* CACHE Advanced Diploma in Child Care and Education
* BTEC Higher National Certificate or Diploma in Early Years Care and Education
* NVQ Level 4 in Early Years Care and Education (England, Wales and Northern Ireland)
* SVQ Level 4 in Early Years Care and Education (Scotland)
* Foundation Degree in Early Childhood Studies.

All applicants for teacher training must have GCSEs in English Language and Mathematics at grade C or above. Applicants born on or after 1 September 1979 who enter primary teacher training also need to achieve a GCSE grade C (or equivalent) in a science subject. There is no upper age limit for entry to teaching training and mature applicants are encouraged. For further information contact the Teacher Training Agency: www.useyourheadteach.gov.uk.

Teaching assistant

A teaching assistant works in a school to assist teachers in the provision of appropriate learning experiences for children. Teaching assistants are based in primary, secondary or special schools. In primary and special schools, teaching assistants may be responsible for supporting one child or a small group of children with special needs, or they may be assigned to work with a particular class. In secondary schools, a teaching assistant usually works with one particular child across all curriculum subjects. There is a range of qualifications available for teaching assistants, especially for those working with young children. Personal qualities, previous relevant experience and appropriate skills are often more important than any specific qualifications. For further information about training as a teaching assistant see: www.teachernet.gov.uk.

> **EXERCISE:** Find out about other job opportunities for working with children in your area.

WORKING ABROAD WITH CHILDREN

There are many jobs available for childcare professionals who wish to work with children abroad. For example:

* au pair working in a private family home
* children's holiday representative supervising children's activity clubs in a holiday resort or on a cruise ship
* nursery nurse or nursery assistant working in a holiday resort crèche or nursery
* private nanny looking after the children of holiday guests in their own chalets or hotel rooms.

Working as an au pair

Jobs working as an au pair are available all year round. Many au pair jobs are for a minimum period of six months to a year, but this may be less for a summer job. Western Europe, Turkey, Israel, USA and Canada have au pair programmes. The Au Pair in America programme is one of the few legal ways for foreigners to work in the USA.

One of the safest ways to work with children abroad is to get employment as an au pair arranged through a recruitment agency. There are many recruitment agencies specializing in placing au pairs with families abroad. An agency can:

* help you sort out any problems with the family
* help you meet other au pairs in the area
* offer advice and support.

Other ways to find work as an au pair include advertisements on the Internet or in newspapers and specialist magazines such as *Nursery World* or *The Lady* (see chapter 3).

The minimum age for working as an au pair is 17 years (18 years in some countries) and the maximum is 27 years. To work as an au pair you must be single, enjoy working with children and be able to do general light housework. Au pairs usually have no formal childcare qualifications and may have little or no experience of caring for children. For the Au Pair in America programme, you must be aged 18–26 years, with childcare experience and a full driving licence.

In European countries, you can expect pocket money of around £30–50 per week, plus full board and lodging. You may be responsible for paying your own study fees, although the family may help you with the travelling costs to college. For the Au Pair in America programme, you can expect around $140 per week, plus full board and lodging, money towards part-time study at a nearby college, work visa, free return flight and medical insurance.

Your duties will include about five hours work per day. Your responsibilities may include:

* waking the children, dressing and bathing them
* preparing light meals or helping to prepare meals and feeding the children
* playing with the children
* making the children's beds, doing their laundry and ironing their clothes
* taking/collecting children to/from school, appointments or outings
* shopping, hoovering, dusting and other light housework
* staying at home while the children are absent from school due to illness or holidays
* babysitting up to two evenings per week.

Remember that an au pair is not a cleaner or a housemaid; your responsibilities do not include heavy housework unrelated to the children, such as cleaning the windows or general cleaning of the family home.

As an au pair you must be given free time daily to study or pursue other interests. In return for carrying out your childcare responsibilities and light housework duties, you can expect one full day off plus study time and other times by arrangement, e.g. any evening when babysitting is not required.

You must be provided with your own bedroom where you can study comfortably. However, you should also be made to feel welcome to share in the social life of the family, as if you were a member of the family. You should join in with family meals and participate in other social activities as invited by the family, e.g. family outings, visits to museums, concerts. This will help to combat any feelings of homesickness and loneliness you may have (see chapter 11).

Working in a holiday resort or on a cruise ship

If you want to work as a children's holiday representative, it is best to go through a recruitment agency who provide staff only for reputable tour operators. The agency should ensure that you:

✳ work no more than 48 hours per week

✳ are paid your wages on time

✳ work with only small groups of children or on a one-to-one basis with babies

✳ have the necessary support to do the job.

The benefits of this type of work include:

✳ free accommodation and free travel

✳ working with different children each week/fortnight

✳ more excitement and variation than the day-to-day routine of working for one family

✳ opportunities to provide a variety of fun and imaginative activities for children.

However, there are some disadvantages to this type of work, such as:

✳ being exploited by some holiday companies or tour operators

✳ poor working conditions (e.g. very long hours – up to 80 hours per week in some cases)

✳ dirty and/or cramped accommodation

✳ too much responsibility (e.g. sole charge of 30 children)

✳ employers may withhold wages or passport to prevent you leaving.

Remember that as well as consulting your recruitment agency, you can always contact the British Embassy, who will be able to provide advice and support if you get into difficulties.

To enjoy working with children in a holiday resort or on a cruise ship you need:

✳ a recognized childcare qualification and experience of working with children

✳ to find out as much as possible about the resort, holiday company and/or tour operator *before* you start work

✳ lots of patience, energy and enthusiasm

✳ plenty of confidence and independence

✳ to be able to make friends easily

✳ to work well as part of a team

✳ a sense of humour!

EXERCISE: Find out about job opportunities for working abroad with children.

Further reading

Griffith, S. and Legg, S., 2002, *The Au Pair and Nanny's Guide to Working Abroad*, 4th edition, Vacation Work Publications.

Humphrics, J., 2000, *Careers Working with Children and Young People*, Kogan Page.

Lifetime Careers, 1998, *Working with Children and Young People*, Hodder and Stoughton.

Question and Answers Career Book, 2001, *Questions and Answers: careers in child care*, Trotman.

Appendix: Useful information

A

Advisory, Conciliation and Arbitration Service (ACAS)
Head Office: Brandon House, 180 Borough High Street, London, SE1 1LW
Tel: 020 7210 3613 Helpline: 08457 474747
Website: www.acas.org.uk

All4KidsUK Ltd
14 The Service Road, Potters Bar, Hertfordshire, EN6 1QA
Tel: 01707 659383
Website: www.all4kidsuk.com
(a comprehensive children's directory for parents and carers)

Amateur Swimming Association
Head Office: ASA, Harold Fern House, Derby Square, Loughborough, LE11 5AL
Tel: 01509 618700
Website: www.britishswimming.org

Ask Nanny
Website: www.ask-nanny.com

B

Best Bear Childcare
Tel: 020 7352 5852
Website: www.bestbear.co.uk
(includes a nationwide listing of recommended childcare agencies)

British Association for Early Childhood Education
136 Cavell Street, London, E1 2JA
Tel: 020 7539 5400
Website: www.early-education.org.uk

British Red Cross
9 Grosvenor Crescent, London, SW1X 7EJ
Tel: 020 7235 5454
Website: www.redcross.org.uk

Bully OnLine
Tel: 01235 212286 (UK National Workplace Bullying Advice Line)
Website: www.bullyonline.org

C

Child Accident Prevention Trust (CAPT)
18–20 Farringdon Lane, London, EC1R 3HA
Tel: 020 7608 3828
Website: www.capt.org.uk

Children's Play Council
National Children's Bureau, 8 Wakley Street, London, EC1V 7QE
Tel: 020 7843 6016
Website: www.ncb.org.uk

Childworks
Weaver House, 19–21 Chapel Road, London, SE27 0TP
Tel: 020 8653 6345
Website: www.childworks.co.uk
(information on jobs in childcare and early years education)

The Chiltern College
16 Peppard Road, Caversham, Reading, RG4 8JZ
Tel: 0118 947 1847
Website: www.chilterncollege.com

Citizen's Advice Bureau (CAB)
Head Office: The National Association of Citizens Advice Bureaux, Myddelton
House, 115–123 Pentonville Road, London, N1 9LZ
Website: www.adviceguide.org.uk

Commission for Racial Equality (CRE)
Head Office: St Dunstan's House, 201–211 Borough High Street, London, SE1 1GZ
Tel: 020 7939 0000 (general enquiries)
Website: www.cre.gov.uk

Council for Awards in Children's Care and Education (CACHE)
8 Chequer Street, St Albans, Hertfordshire, AL1 3XZ
Tel: 01727 847636
Website: www.cache.org.uk

Criminal Records Bureau (CRB)
Information line: 0870 909 0811
Website: www.crb.gov.uk
Disclosures website: www.disclosure.gov.uk

Cruse Bereavement Care
Central Office: Cruse House, 126 Sheen Road, Richmond, Surrey, TW9 1UR
Tel: 0870 167 1677 (helpline)
Website: www.crusebereavementcare.org.uk

D

Days Out Atlas Online
St Faiths House, Mountergate, Norwich, Norfolk, NR1 1PY
Tel: 01603 633808
Website: www.daysoutatlas.co.uk

Department for Education & Skills (DfES)
Sanctuary Buildings, Great Smith Street, London, SW1P 3BT
Tel: 0870 000 2288
Website: www.dfes.gov.uk (homepage) and
www.surestart.gov.uk/ensuringquality/needananny/

Department for Work and Pensions (DWP)
Correspondence Unit, Room 540, The Adelphi, 1–11 John Adam Street,
London, WC2N 6HT
Tel: 020 7712 2171
Website: www.dwp.gov.uk

Disability Rights Commission (DRC)
DRC Helpline, Freepost MID02164, Stratford upon Avon, CV37 9BR
Helpline: 08457 622633 Textphone: 08457 622644
Website: www.drc-gb.org

Disability Information Centre
Middlesborough General Hospital, Ayresome Green Lane,
Middlesborough, TS5 5AZ
Tel: 01642 827471

E

Edexcel
Head Office: Stewart House, 32 Russell Square, London, WC1B 5DN
Tel: 0870 240 9800 (customer services)
Website: www.edexcel.org.uk

Educational Visits UK
Elmtree Press, Bedale, North Yorkshire, DL8 2HD
Tel: 01677 427334
Website: www.educationalvisitsuk.com

Equal Opportunities Commission
Arndale House, Arndale Centre, Manchester, M4 3EQ
Tel: 0845 601 5901 (general enquiries)
Website: www.eoc.org.uk

F

4Children
2nd Bellerive House, 3 Muirfield Crescent, London, E14 9SZ
Tel: 020 7512 2112
Website: www.4children.org.uk

G

Greatcare.co.uk
79 Battersea Business Centre, 99–109 Lavender Hill, London, SW11 5QL
Tel: 020 7924 6660
Website: www.greatcare.co.uk
(includes a nanny agency directory for childcare jobs in London and the UK)

Games For Kids
Website: www.links4kids.co.uk/games
(contains links to websites with educational games and fun activities for children)

H

Holiday Resort Jobs
Website: www.holidayresortjobs.co.uk

I

The International Nanny Association
191 Clarksville Road, Princeton Junction, NJ 08550-3111, USA
Tel: 001 609 799 7527 (international number)
Website: www.nanny.org

J

Jobs in Europe
Website: www.jobs-in-Europe.net
(includes links to nanny and au pair agencies in Europe and websites offering information for au pairs on selection criteria, work permits etc.)

K

Kidscape
2 Grosvenor Gardens, London, SW1W 0DH
Tel: 020 7730 3300
Website: www.kidscape.org.uk
(the national charity to help prevent bullying and child abuse)

L

The Lady
39–40 Bedford Street, London, WC2E 9ER
Tel: 020 7379 4717
Website: www.ladymagazine.com

The Law Centres Federation
Duchess House, 18–19 Warren Street, London W1T 5LR
Tel: 020 7387 8570
Website: www.lawcentres.org.uk
(free and independent professional legal advice)

M

Maternity and Nanny Training (MNT)
54 Saffron Close, Chineham, Hampshire, RG24 8XQ
Tel: 0870 2202657
Website: www.mynannynetwork.co.uk

Montessori Centre International
18 Balderton Street, London, W1K 6TG
Tel: 020 7493 0165
Website: www.montessori.ac.uk

N

Nannies at Work Limited
Box 492, 28 Old Brompton Road, London, SW7 3SS
Website: www.nanniesatwork.co.uk

Nanny job
Website: www.nannyjob.co.uk
(free Internet childcare recruitment site)

Nanny Tax
PO Box 988, Brighton, BN1 3NT
Tel: 0845 226 2203
Website: www.nannytax.co.uk

National Early Years Network
77 Holloway Road, London, N7 8JZ
Tel: 020 7607 9573
Website: www.neyn.org.uk
(provides practical support for childcare and early years workers)

National Family and Parenting Institute
430 Highgate Studios, 53–79 Highgate Road, London, NW5 1TL
Tel: 020 7424 3460
Website: www.nfpi.org.uk

National Playing Fields Association (NPFA)
Head Office: Stanley House, St Chad's Place, London, WC1X 9HH
Tel: 020 7833 5360
Website: www.playing-fields.com

National Society for the Prevention of Cruelty to Children (NSPCC)
Weston House, 42 Curtain Road, London, EC2A 3NH
Tel: 020 7825 2500 NSPCC Child Protection Helpline: 0808 800 5000 (24 hours)
Website: www.nspcc.org.uk

Norland College
York Place, London Road, Bath, BA1 6AE
Tel: 01225 466202
Website: www.norland.co.uk

Nursery World
Admiral House, 66–68 East Smithfield, London, E1W 1BX
Tel: 020 7782 3000
Website: www.nursery-world.com

O

Office for Standards in Education (Ofsted)
Alexandra House, 33 Kingsway, London, WC2B 6SE
Tel: 020 7421 6800 Helpline: 08456 014771
Website: www.ofsted.gov.uk

P

Pre-school Learning Alliance
London Head Office: Unit 213–216, 30 Great Guildford Street, London, SE1 0HS
Tel: 020 7620 0550
Website: www.pre-school.org.uk

Professional Association of Nursery Nurses (PANN)
2 St James' Court, Friar Gate, Derby, DE1 1BT
Tel: 01332 372337
Website: www.pat.org.uk

Q

Queen Elizabeth's Foundation for Disabled People
Leatherhead Court, Woodlands Road, Leatherhead, Surrey, KT22 0BN
Tel: 01372 841100
Website: www.qefd.org

R

Recruitment and Employment Confederation (REC)
36–38 Mortimer Street, London, W1W 7RG
Tel: 020 7462 3260
Website: www.rec.uk.com
(has Code of Practice for Childcare Agencies)

Royal Society for the Prevention of Accidents (RoSPA)
Edgbaston Park, 353 Bristol Road, Birmingham, B5 7ST
Tel: 0121 248 2000 (general information)
Website: www.rospa.com

S

St. John Ambulance
27 St. John's Lane, London, EC1M 4BU
Tel: 08700 104950
Website: www.sja.org.uk

T

Trades Union Congress (TUC)
Congress House, Great Russell Street, London, WC1B 3LS
Tel: 020 7636 4030 (general enquires) 0870 600 4882 (rights line)
Website: www.tuc.org.uk (for comprehensive information on many work-related issues)

Traveline
Public transport information
Tel: 0870 6082608
Website: www.traveline.org.uk
(impartial information on planning your journey, by bus, coach or train)

U

Under5s
PO Box 137, Ilkley, West Yorkshire, LS29 7AH
Tel: 01943 604561 (24-hour answerphone)
Website: www.underfives.co.uk
(resources and information for early years education)

V

Volunteering England
Regents Wharf, 8 All Saints Street, London N1 9RL
Tel: 0800 028 3304
Website: www.navb.org.uk

W

Winston's Wish
Clara Burgess Centre, Bayshill Road, Cheltenham, GL50 3AW
Tel: 0845 2030405
Website: www.winstonswish.org.uk
(support for bereaved children and their parents or carers)

Women's Aid Federation of England
PO Box 391, Bristol, BS99 7WS
Helpline: 0808 2000 247 (freephone 24 hours)
website: www.womensaid.org.uk
(a national charity offering support, advice and information on domestic violence)

X

Xchange
Website: www.bbc.co.uk/xchange
(contains games and fun activities for children plus links to other BBC websites for children, including CBeebies)

Y

Young Explorers
Website: www.youngexplorers.co.uk
(lists detailed information on books about family holidays and travelling with children)

Z

Zoo directory
Website: www.ukwebfind.co.uk/placestogo.html
(lists zoos, safari parks, wildlife parks, sea life centres, theme parks, castles, museums, art galleries and other attractions suitable for children)

Bibliography

Allen, J. (ed.), 2003, 'Time to act over nannies', '*The Nanny State*' supplement in *Early Years Educator*, vol. 5, no. 7, November.

Bartholomew, L. and Bruce, T., 1993, *Getting To Know You: a guide to record-keeping in early childhood education and care*, London: Hodder and Stoughton.

Breese, C. and Gomer, H., 1993, *The Good Nanny Guide: the complete handbook on nannies, au-pairs, mother's helps and childminders*, 3rd edition, London: Vermilion.

Bruce, T. and Meggitt, C., 2002, *Child Care and Education*, 3rd edition, London: Hodder and Stoughton.

Child Accident Prevention Trust, 2002a, *Fact Sheet: home accidents*, London: Child Accident Prevention Trust.

Child Accident Prevention Trust, 2002b, *Fact Sheet: toys and accidents*, London: Child Accident Prevention Trust.

Davenport, C., 1994, *An Introduction to Child Development*, London: Collins Educational.

Davie, R., 1994, 'Social development and social behaviour', in Fontana, D. (ed.), *The Education of the Young Child*, Oxford: Blackwell.

Department for Education and Skills, 2004, *Need a Nanny? A guide for parents*, London: DfES.

Department of Health, 1991, *The Children Act 1989: Guidance and regulations, Volume 2: Family support, day care and educational provision and young children*, London: HMSO.

Department of Health, the Home Office and the Department for Education, 1999, *Working Together To Safeguard Children*, London: HMSO.

Donaldson, M., 1978, *Children's Minds*, London: Fontana.

Einon, D., 1986, *Creative Play*, London: Penguin.

Fontana, D., 1994, 'Personality and personal development', in Fontana, D. (ed.), *The Education of the Young Child*, Oxford: Blackwell.

Foster-Cohen, S., 1999, *Introduction to Child Language Development*, Harlow: Longman.

Gathorne-Hardy, J., 1972, *The Rise and Fall of the British Nanny*, London: Hodder and Stoughton.

Gibson, F., 2003, 'Nappy-changing, baby-sitting – and lots of testosterone. Meet the manny…', *The Observer*, 23 March.

Goleman, D., 1996, *Emotional Intelligence*, London: Bloomsbury.

Green, C., 1990, *Toddler Taming: a parents' guide to the first four years*, London: Vermilion.

Griffith, S. and Legg, S., 2002, *The Au Pair and Nanny's Guide to Working Abroad*, 4th edition, Oxford: Vacation Work.

Hines, D., 2002, *Resolving Conflict in Marriage*, Pittsburgh, PA: Whitaker House.

Hinsliff, G., 2003, 'It's who cares wins for the male nanny', *The Observer*, 9 March.

Houghton, D. and McColgan, M., 1995, *Working with Children*, London: Collins Educational.

Humphries, S., Mack, J. and Perks, R., 1988, *A Century of Childhood*, London: Sidgwick & Jackson in association with Channel Four Television Company.

Hutchcroft, D., 1981, *Making Language Work*, London: McGraw-Hill.

Kamen, T., 2000, *Psychology for Childhood Studies*, London: Hodder and Stoughton.

Laing, A. and Chazan, M., 1994, 'Young children with special educational needs', in Fontana, D. (ed.), *The Education of the Young Child*, Oxford: Blackwell.

Lindon, J., 1997, *Working with Young Children*, 3rd edition, London: Edward Arnold.

Leach, P., 1994, *Children First*, London: Penguin.

Lee, V. and Das Gupta, P. (eds.), 1995, *Children's Cognitive and Language Development*, Oxford: Blackwell.

Light, P., Sheldon, S. and Woodhead, M. (eds.), 1991, *Learning To Think*, London: Routledge.

Lindenfield, G., 1995, *Self-esteem*, London: Thorsons.

Marten, S., 1997, *Careers in Child Care: your questions and answers*, Richmond, Surrey: Trotman and Company Limited.

Masheder, M., 1989, *Let's Play Together*, London: Green Print.

Matterson, E., 1989, *Play with a Purpose for the Under-sevens*, London: Penguin.

Meadows, S., 1993, *Child as Thinker: the development of cognition in childhood*, London: Routledge.

Mort, L. and Morris, J., 1989, *Bright Ideas for Early Years: getting started*, London: Scholastic.

Moyle, D., 1976, *The Teaching of Reading*, London: Ward Lock Educational.

Mulvaney, A., 1995, *Talking with Kids*, Sydney: Simon & Schuster.

Neaum, S. and Tallack, J., 1997, *Good Practice in Implementing the Pre-school Curriculum*, London: Stanley Thornes.

NFPI, October 2003, *Fact Sheet 3 – Work and the Family Today: an at-a-glance guide*, 3rd edition, London: National Family and Parenting Institute.

Nilsdotter, A., 2003, 'Net tax effect is a gross loss', *'The Nanny State'* supplement in *Early Years Educator*, vol. 5, no. 7, November.

Oliver, I., 2000, *Ideas for PSHE*, Leamington Spa: Scholastic Limited.

Petrie, P., 1989, *Communicating with Children and Adults*, London: Edward Arnold.

Qualifications and Curriculum Authority, 2000, *Curriculum Guidance for the Foundation Stage*, London: QCA.

Royal College of Psychiatrists, 2002, *Child Abuse and Neglect – the emotional effects*, Fact Sheet 20 (for parents and teachers), London: Royal College of Psychiatrists.

Stoppard, M., 1990, *The New Baby Care Book*, London: Dorling Kindersley.

Taylor, J., 1973, *Reading and Writing in the First School*, London: George Allen and Unwin.

Tough, J., 1976, *Listening to Children Talking*, London: Ward Lock Educational.

Tough, J., 1994, 'How young children develop and use language', in Fontana, D. (ed.), *The Education of the Young Child*, Oxford: Blackwell.

Train, A., 1996, *ADHD: how to deal with very difficult children*, London: Souvenir Press.

Watkinson, A., 2003, *The Essential Guide for Competent Teaching Assistants*, London: David Fulton Publishers.

Whitehead, M., 1996, *The Development of Language and Literacy*, London: Hodder and Stoughton.

Wood, D., 1988, *How Children Think and Learn*, Oxford: Blackwell.

Woolfson, R., 1989, *Understanding your Child: a parents' guide to child psychology*, London: Faber & Faber.

Woolfson, R., 1991, *Children with Special Needs: a guide for parents and carers*, London: Faber & Faber.

Yardley, A., 1994, 'Understanding and encouraging children's play', in Fontana, D. (ed.), *The Education of the Young Child*, Oxford: Blackwell.

Yeo, A. and Lovell, T., 2002, *Sociology and Social Policy for the Early Years*, 2nd edition, London: Hodder and Stoughton.

Index